What Others Are Say

Parkinson's disease creeps into many lives with little fanfare. It arrives as an accumulation of almost unnoticed changes over time, each bothersome in its own way, but can often be shrugged off as "just getting older." Eventually those changes compound, and can no longer be hidden. Or ignored. And when the official diagnosis is presented, many ask, "Why me?

Rick's discovery of the truth, that he had a chronic and progressive disease that would change how he lived, could have been devastating. It tested his faith. Because his faith is at the center of his life, Rick turned to prayer and meditation.

Rick encountered the full catastrophe of Parkinson's disease, and used that catastrophe to bolster his faith, even to find gratitude in the daily challenges. Rick invited his family and friends in his mission to live a full and fruitful life. Through prayer, he found that part of his strategy to lead a life of wellness was to help teach others with the disease how to build a full life. His story is inspiring to everyone who will confront a chronic and progressive life challenge.

—**Chris Gaffney**, Executive Director,
Parkinson Support and Wellness

Rick intricately outlines life stories with practical use of biblical references, bringing the reader a greater understanding of the "why me" moments. The stories and lessons are easily relatable to any reader. Well-detailed, causing a connection to the author. Rick beautifully highlights the ebbs and flows, trials and tribulations, and the victories of a progressive and unpredictable disease process. Uplifting and well written.

—**Caitlin Fattore**, MS, CCC-SLP,
Voices for Parkinson's Inc

In life, Rick has taught me how to find joy in the everyday moments and to search for the good in all things and all people. I am sure this book will inspire you to follow those same principles. It was a joy to read Rick's words and to hear them in his voice.

—**Becca Metz**, Physical Therapist

What Others Are Saying About This Book

As a retired family medicine physician, I have often reflected on the many patients I have seen who were given an incurable diagnosis and their life journey after that diagnosis. This book portrays the journey of Rick, who was given the diagnosis of Parkinson's disease at an early adult age. Rick's story shows us his courage, strength, tenacity, and his strong faith in God and His providence. Rick shows us it is even ok to ask God some of those hard questions and wait for an answer. Anyone facing an incurable illness or other life challenge would be blessed by reading this book, seeing how one man, through God's grace and mercy, has kept the journey going.

—**Gary Melton**, MD

It is unknown how or why God allows the circumstances in our lives that cause us pain and suffering. The solace is that we "join Him in his suffering" so we can become more like Him. In Rick's new book, *My Gift From God: Parkinson's Disease,* our hearts are touched, our minds opened, to answer the questions of why, how, and what. Through Rick's candid recount of his struggles, we gain courage and confidence to push ahead and to endure. A memoir of inspirational honesty and vulnerability. A testament to grace and resolve, humility, and compassion. A privilege to read.

—**DeeDee Schnetzer**, Friend

Rick shares this raw story of his Parkinson's journey with incredible vulnerability. He recounts his trials—all of them—with faith, and even joy. He puts his WHOLE life in God's hands, allowing him to accept God's purpose for his life, even through his many challenges. As he journeys on through his disease, he sees God's love so fiercely through friends, family, and circumstance. Having the good fortune to know Rick personally, he not only tells his story so vividly through writing, he lives it everyday! An incredible read; uplifting, encouraging, and hopeful!

—**Maureen Scheiner,** Boxing Instructor

What Others Are Saying About This Book

Rick's book tells the personal story of an individual whose deep religious faith has provided guidance and support in his journey to deal with the challenges of a difficult and debilitating disease while continuing to serve the community of others with the disease, through his fundraising efforts. His indomitable spirit in dealing with his disease and huge commitment to meet stretching fundraising goals is inspiring.

—**Dave Ebner**, Board Member,
Steady Strides 5K Fundraising Race

Isaiah 12:3 reminds us that "With joy we will draw water from the wells of salvation" … Rick's book takes us on a very personal journey of pain and suffering … and redemption … it's a glimpse into the life of an "overcomer" that serves to empower the reader to trust again even when their world seems to be falling apart … to "give thanks in ALL things" … to receive the "water" … (the nourishment, wisdom and purpose) that can only come from God.

Chronic illnesses have the capacity to leave us feeling abandoned and insignificant … like a "broken doll" or an injured deer along the highway.

Rick's raw testimony hits you right in the gut … all of a sudden you feel yourself in the "pit" of despair along with him … But his words of faith ring true to the man … they are ingrained in Rick's very soul.

Walk this journey with Rick and you will find a new font of courage and resolve.

Thank you, friend, for sharing your heart in such an intimate and encouraging way.

—**Dottie Dunn**, RN

What Others Are Saying About This Book

Rick's book is definitely a must read for everyone. It is very inspirational and engaging as Rick speaks of the relationship he develops with his friend, Larry. At the same time, we appreciate the discussion of the power of positivity and prayer when dealing with difficult issues. We are looking forward to reading the additional chapters. We thoroughly recommend it.

—**Bob Wetterer,** Realtor,
Comey and Shepherd
—**Nancy Wetterer,** Office Administrator,
Parkinson Support &Wellness

You will be inspired and encouraged as you read this book. At the beginning, Rick asks, "Can anything good come from Parkinson's?" The contents of this book answer that question in terms of grace and hope, as we see that, even with Parkinson's or whatever our "Parkinson's" might be, "God will give His gift of grace to bear it."

—**Patti Boehnlein,** Running Teammate and Friend

Rick states that he is a blessed man who happens to have Parkinson's. I see in these pages a man who wants to share that blessing with others through this penetrating look into the physical and spiritual realities of his very personal Parkinson's journey. I could hear Rick talking as I read his words, and I could see him crossing the finish line numerous times at the race. It makes me think of the numerous and varied finish lines just waiting for him to cross as he continues his journey.

—**Jack Boehnlein,** Running Teammate and Friend

The author views Parkinson's disease not as a curse, but rather as a gift from God. This perspective has made him an "overcomer." He embraces the opportunities presented by life with a chronic illness and hopes to thereby inspire and encourage others.

—**Elizabeth Grover**, Vice President,
Parkinson Support & Wellness

My Gift from God: Parkinson's Disease

Richard A. Iles

My Gift From God: Parkinson's Disease

Richard A. Iles

WINTERS
PUBLISHING

winterspublishing.com

To purchase a copy of this book
or to contact the author, please email at:

iles_foley@yahoo.com

© 2023 by Rick Iles.

Cover design by Michael Iles

Winters Publishing
P.O. Box 501
Greensburg, IN 47240
812-663-4948
www.winterspublishing.com

Library of Congress Control Number: 2022948317
ISBN: 978-1-954116-14-6

Printed in the United States of America.

Dedicated to:

My wife, Terri;

my children—Philip, Michael, Amy, and Debra;

and their families

The leadership team at the Parkinson

Support & Wellness Organization

Parkinson's patients, their caregivers,

and their families and friends

Table of Contents

Table of Contents (continued)

Part 4
Down, But Not Out

Foreword

During our last clinic visit, I was excited to learn from Rick Iles that he had authored another book, *My Gift From God: Parkinson's Disease*. Rick became a patient of mine in 2005, only a couple of months after my arrival to Cincinnati. Since our very first encounter, Rick struck me as someone who was not going to let this newly-discovered thing in his life, Parkinson's, define him. Not a chance.

Over the years, instead, he has come to redefine Parkinson's, at least for me, with his resilience, creativity, perseverance, and faith. The pages that follow illustrate the many ways in which he has accomplished it—and what he means by Parkinson's as a gift.

Early on, Rick had to overcome several troublesome aspects of the brand of Parkinson's he developed. Nowhere was this challenge greater than in the form of impaired regulation of his blood pressure, one of the many problems that can appear in this disease. Just when I thought we had exhausted all possible tools to correct this problem and was considering the extreme decision to enroll him in a clinical trial of an experimental medication, somehow, miraculously, this problem vanished. It has only rarely reappeared since.

This was one of several examples that led me to believe in Rick's uniqueness. It's only fitting for him to have compiled the most salient stories in this memoir, which will surely become an inspirational source to many. Rick is a spiritual man. His experience with Parkinson's has been deeply affected by his belief in God. This is rendered transparently clear in the many improbable stories he recounts. My personal favorite is the one gracing the pages of Chapter 8. He had developed foot dystonia, a twisting, sometimes painful posturing of a foot, which can affect the ability to walk. How he came upon the WalkAide® is the result of what can only be described as divine intervention!

The Parkinson's disease that Rick came to show is not the one I necessarily predicted when I met him over sixteen years ago. But his belief in God, his dedication to work, his commitment to exercise, his positive attitude, and the bottomless support of his kind wife, Terri, combined to buckle any odds against him. He knew it would all work out, somehow—always inspired by the wisdom of the biblical scriptures that are as sprinkled in his life as they are in this book. Rick tamed the beast of Parkinson's into something that had no chance to define him—and something that only made him stronger.

Rick's approach to living with Parkinson's, he has taught me, is one way to defeat it. This book is also a testament to the power of faith and love in turning adversities into opportunities. I shall forever treasure *My Gift From God: Parkinson's Disease.*

Alberto J. Espay, MD, MSc, FAAN

Professor of Neurology
Director and Endowed Chair
Gardner Family Center for Parkinson's Disease
    and Movement Disorders
University of Cincinnati
February 23, 2022

Dr. Alberto Espay and Rick.

Introduction

What Does God Want to Say Through You?

Teach me to do your will, for you are my God;
may your good Spirit lead me on level ground.
Psalm 143:10

As iron sharpens iron,
so one person sharpens another.
Proverbs 27:17

"What?! You have a lot to say," my friend Larry Blundred shouted at me. We had been meeting two or three times a month for the past eight years. In 2012, his wife, Donna, was diagnosed with a brain tumor and was given six months to live. As Larry struggled to accept this diagnosis, he began to share the burdens of his heart. We met to pray, study God's Word, discuss our daily devotions, and open our hearts to each other. We became accountable to each other, and as iron sharpens iron, we became better men because of our friendship.

In 2017, Larry published a book titled *Staying Resilient When Life Throws You A Curveball*. It described the many changes his family was going through as a result of Donna's diagnosis. It included his own spiritual struggles and growth as he dealt with his wife having a brain tumor. Her story of surviving and thriving in the face of many challenges was remarkable. She was still alive five years later. When we met, we discussed how she met each challenge head on and constantly beat the odds.

Larry told me I should write my story of being diagnosed with Parkinson's disease, a progressive, degenerative, incurable, chronic illness. I had been fighting it for sixteen years. Larry believed my story showed that an ordinary man, with no claim to fame, could be used by God in an extraordinary way. Every time Larry brought it up, I responded, "I don't have anything to say." Larry always replied, "You have a lot to say." I was good at talking one-on-one with people, but what did I have to say that other people would want to hear. *Nothing*, I thought.

In October of 2017 when I gave my usual reply, Larry startled me by exploding with exasperation and frustration. He looked me in the eye, clenched his teeth, and exclaimed, "What?! Look at this notebook I've been keeping. It is full of things you have to say. But, the real question is this: *What does God want to say through you?*"

That was the moment the rubber met the road. I realized Larry was challenging me by questioning my commitment to the Lord. Larry continued his little speech: "Are you willing to be obedient to the prompting of the Holy Spirit on your heart? Will you pray about it and intentionally do what God tells you to do?" I wanted to say, "Bug Off! Who died and left you in charge?" But my response was, "Yes, I'll pray about it." What else could I say? As he walked out the door he turned and said, "Write."

After Larry left, I reread the chapter of his book titled *Writing Your Story*. As I read, the still, small voice of the Holy Spirit whispered, "This is a journey I want you to take. This journey will be hard for you, but I will lead you and direct you. I will put people in your life who need to hear your story. Never stop believing this. I told you sixteen years ago I would cover you just as I had covered my landscape with a light snow. I haven't changed. I'm still covering you, guiding you, leading you, and walking with you as you begin this new journey. Yield to my will and follow me on this incredible adventure I have planned for you."

"This is a completely different type of journey than you would plan. My Word describes it this way: 'Although the Lord gives you the bread of adversity, and the water of affliction, your teachers will be hidden no more, with your own eyes you will see them. Whether you turn to the right or to the left, your ears will hear a voice behind you, saying, This is the way, walk in it'" (Isaiah 30:20–21). Then He said, "I've given you two gifts: Parkinson's disease and the gift of writing. Go and write your story about the blessings of living with Parkinson's disease."

I wanted to say to the Lord the same thing I had thought about saying to Larry, "Bug Off! Who died and left you in charge?" But I wouldn't dare say that out loud to God. After a prolonged period of silence, God, who knew my every thought, spoke. "I died, and I am in charge. Here is the title for the book: *My Gift From God: Parkinson's Disease.*" Then I heard a quiet, tender whisper as God said, "Be obedient. Go write."

PART 1

HANGING ON FOR DEAR LIFE

CHAPTERS 1–5

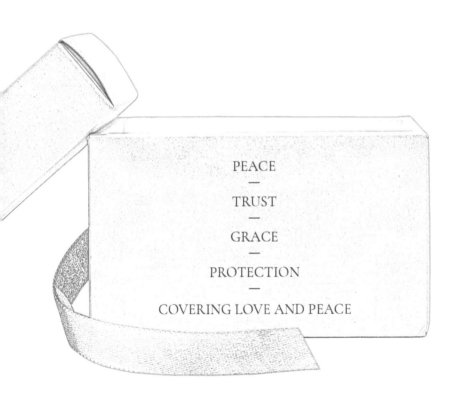

PEACE

—

TRUST

—

GRACE

—

PROTECTION

—

COVERING LOVE AND PEACE

Chapter 1

Bewildered: I'll Ignore the Symptoms

Trust in him at all times,
you people; pour out your hearts to him,
for God is our refuge.
Psalm 62:8

Peace I leave with you;
my peace I give you …
John 14:27

In November 2003, I had tremors in my hands. I noticed them when I was hunting and while butchering a deer. Terri, my wife, also saw them and wondered if it was Parkinson's disease. The tremors continued and worsened over the next year and a half. During that time, I developed dystonia (a movement disorder in which the muscles contract uncontrollably) in my left foot.

In April and May of 2005, other symptoms appeared. I had facial tremors, muscle spasms, and could not smile. I began to drool. Movement became slow, with fine motor skills rapidly disappearing. My back, shoulders, and neck were very stiff. All of these symptoms resulted in extreme fatigue.

I feared I might have cancer, a brain tumor, or multiple sclerosis (MS). I was too young to be really sick. I didn't talk to Terri about it. I prayed the symptoms would go away. Gary, my brother-in-law and a doctor, noticed my stiffness, slow movement, lack of energy, and tremors. He told me to see a neurologist. I knew I should, but I couldn't muster up the courage to call. I simply didn't want to hear the prognosis.

In June 2005, Terri and I chaperoned a group of teenagers at the Alive Music Festival in Akron, Ohio. I couldn't get my left hand to wave goodbye to Shepherd, the youth director's young son. One afternoon while walking to a concert, Terri and I shared our fears that something was drastically wrong with me. We discussed several of my symptoms: diminishing fine motor skills, stiffness, my speech not keeping up with my brain, arm pain, trouble walking, and feeling like I'm going to fall.

I wanted to ignore it so it would go away, and yet I wanted to know what it was so I could deal with it. We were scared. I thought about my dad who had died from bone cancer, and wondered if Terri would have to take care of me for a few years and then live as a widow, like my mother. Chasing these thoughts away, I prayed, "Lord, give me peace."

We returned from the Alive Festival and began to finalize our plans for Camp Chazon, a church camp where I was a co-director. We had three weeks to prepare before it started on Monday, July 11. During this time I was very emotional. I would cry about little things, but then be singing ten minutes later. I was a mixed bag of emotions. I felt like I had climbed on board a roller coaster and I was experiencing the highs, lows, and loops of this wild ride. This was new to me. But up or down, fast or slow, life must go on, so off to camp I went.

I had a hard time at Monday's registration. I couldn't think quickly and had difficulty problem solving. I began to stutter because my mouth couldn't keep up with my brain. On Tuesday I was extremely fatigued and stayed in bed almost the whole day. I left camp on Wednesday morning.

I spent the next two days at home in bed. I was physically and emotionally exhausted. I prayed several times the Lord would heal me even though I didn't know what was wrong. I asked the Lord to help me accept whatever He had planned for my life. I prayed this simple prayer many times: "Lord, please do what is best for me and best for Your Kingdom."

Junior camp began a week after senior camp. By then, I thought I was feeling good enough to attend camp and run the program. However, on Monday morning as I was checking the campers in, I had trouble thinking quickly and formulating sentences. Charlie, the co-director, noticed. He insisted that if I stayed all week, I had to take a nap every afternoon.

Terri arrived later that day. After we unloaded her car, she told me she had made an appointment for me to see a neurologist who specialized in Parkinson's disease. I hid it from her, but it crushed me because I knew she thought something was really wrong with me.

As the week progressed, my fatigue returned. I had no patience with these young campers who needed lots of attention. But I was determined to maintain a good attitude even though it was a long week. I was glad when it was over.

On August 1, I attended a funeral and saw several of the teachers I worked with. I must have looked terrible. I know I *felt* terrible. Peggy Sparks, the librarian at our school, gruffly told me I should be in the hospital where the doctors could figure out what was wrong with me. It made me a little angry she was harsh with me in front of my friends, interrupting our conversation. As I had with Larry, I wanted to say to her, "Bug Off! Who died and left you in charge?" She stopped by my house that afternoon and apologized for being so gruff with me. But before she left, she was very harsh again as she told me to get to the hospital. It was hard to get mad at her because I knew she loved me and was really worried about me.

The next week, we decided to go to Indianapolis and visit Phill and Rita Frye, our best friends for fifty-two years. Our youngest daughter, Debra, went with us, so I sat in the back seat of the car. Without Terri knowing it, I made a list of symptoms I had been experiencing for the past few months. I figured we would discuss these symptoms when we arrived at the Frye's. But as soon as we got there, Phill told me that Shane, his oldest son, fell off a ladder and broke his leg. Phill and I headed for the hospital.

While we were waiting for the doctor to come out and tell us the extent of Shane's injury, Phill asked about my health. It was obvious that something was wrong with me. I verbalized that Terri thought I had Parkinson's disease. This was hard because I feared that she was right. Phill showed me what a true friend looks like when he said, "Whatever it is that's wrong, I'll be there for you and we will deal with it together." I wondered why he would choose to suffer with me. I thanked the Lord that my friend was willing to walk down this road with me, even if the road turned out to be a steep, windy, gravel road with many potholes.

When Terri and I got home, we were invited by some friends to a horse farm for an afternoon picnic and some riding. While we were there, several people talked to me about my health. It seemed everyone was beginning to notice something was wrong. What was it? I wanted to know, yet I didn't want to know. I talked to the Lord about being able to deal with whatever was wrong. As I listened to my friends talk about my health, I was amazed at how calmly I received their observations. It was as if they were pointing at me, but talking about someone else. Denial is a wonderful thing.

When we got home from the picnic, Terri printed a list of Parkinson's symptoms she found on the internet. I compared her list to the list I had written on the way to the Frye's. The truth hit me. I was going to be diagnosed with Parkinson's disease. This put me in a state of bewilderment. I truly believed God wanted what was best for me, but found it hard to see that Parkinson's disease was the best thing for me. I didn't think I could be thankful in this crisis.

Over the next few days, I realized I needed to live out my faith and trust God wholeheartedly. I knew He would replace my fears with the gift of His peace. Even though I believed I could and would receive this gift of peace, I wondered how I would react when the neurologist diagnosed me with Parkinson's disease.

PEACE

Chapter 2

Diagnosis: A Long, Lonely Day

Be still before the LORD and wait patiently for him; ...
Psalm 37:7

Commit your way to the LORD; trust in him
and he will do this:
Psalm 37:5

On Tuesday, August 23, 2005, I saw Dr. George Mandybar. After about ten minutes of discussion, he said he knew what was wrong with me. Terri said, "He has Parkinson's, doesn't he?" The answer was, "Yes, he does." I melted inside, but held my composure during the rest of the visit.

When we got back to the car, Terri asked me how I felt. "I just feel like crying." And then I did. Terri reached for my hand and began to cry. I cried for her. I was like my dad in that I wanted to be the one to care for my wife, not be the one who needed care. What would she deal with in the long run? I knew the disease would be a life-changer and a dream-changer for us. The hope that we would stay healthy and grow old together was shattered, as was my dream of living in a log cabin in the woods.

As we drove home, I told Terri there were only two things I wanted to do that evening. I wanted to see my mother and feel her hug. I also wanted to be alone, to be still before God, talk to Him, and listen for His voice. I had a lot of questions for Him. Terri told me to go and visit my mom. She thought my mom would like to see me, and the drive would give me time to be alone. We ate supper together and I left.

As I drove to Mom's, I cried and talked to God. I wondered how this could be good for me and be good for His Kingdom? Would I get any better? Would I be able to teach? I wanted to be a really great Grandpa. Would I be able to hold Ava, my soon-to-be-born granddaughter, two years from now? Would I be able to catch her when she jumped into my arms, take her on hikes, teach her to fish, and read her a story?

As I turned onto my Mom's road, it seemed I had driven into the middle of a beautiful sunset. There were reddish clouds, some puffy and some long and thin, backed by gorgeous streaks of deep blue. It was God's handwriting spread across the whole expanse of the sky.

God spoke to my heart. "I know. I ordained this. I love you. I will give you the gift of trust and I will use you in the physical state I put you in. Submit to My plan and I will chisel you into the man I want you to be." I listened intently as God spoke to me and then I prayed, "Father, I want to crawl up in Your lap, feel Your arms around me, and just be still in Your presence."

When I arrived at Mom's, she cried and said, "I knew." I melted in her hug and thought, *It's not right. It's just not right! But, it's not something worse.* I also thought about not being whole physically. What a change for me, the "old man" who could always play with his six younger brothers. Perpetually young. Then I cried for myself.

When I went to bed that night, it hit me again. My fear had been confirmed. I had been diagnosed with Parkinson's disease. I was fifty-three years old, but I felt and walked like a much older person. To hear the doctor say the word *Parkinson's* cut to the bone. The hope that it might not be Parkinson's was crushed and blown away. My heart cried out to the Lord, "Oh, God, why? And yet, why not me?" That night I continued to cry: for myself, for Terri, and for my family and friends who would suffer with me.

As the weeks and months went by, I realized I was still riding on the wild and scary roller coaster. I had hopped on board before I was officially diagnosed with Parkinson's. As my symptoms worsened it seemed like I was picking up extra speed each time I went down another steep hill. I was afraid, wondering how I would react when the symptoms of Parkinson's, combined with the challenges, problems, and unexpected events of just an ordinary life, would cause the car to reach breakneck speed and jump the track. As I went faster and faster, my anxiety and stress threatened to take control. But I was determined not to let Parkinson's become the driving force of my life.

I learned the ups and downs on a roller coaster-life could be just minutes apart. Other times, they might be an hour or even a few days apart. Something good would occur and I would be thankful. Then something bad would happen and I would be bewildered. I was surprised that my attitude played such a huge part in how fast the roller coaster moved. I was caught off guard by the different emotions that accompany this illness. Sometimes I feared the roller coaster car was going to come off its track. My prayers were something like this: "Lord, I finally know what is wrong. I'm glad it's not cancer. However, I'm not overjoyed that I have Parkinson's disease. I'm choosing to trust You and to praise You, no matter what comes my way. I won't readily embrace what I call the bad, but I still trust You. Please continue to remind me just how trustworthy You really are."

I felt like my life was a roller coaster ride.

I knew there would be storms in my life, and I knew there would be beautiful days with bright sunlight. Some days Parkinson's disease would be my friend, and other days it would be my foe. I believe, deep in my soul where God dwells, He knows what is best for me. Whatever He has allowed in my life can be a growing point. I prayed, "Lord help me, especially during the bad days, to understand You are in control and You will do what is best for me. Please take me off the roller coaster ride and enable my questioning heart to trust You and to accept Your plan for my life."

Chapter 3

A Runaway Roller Coaster Ride

… "My grace is sufficient for you,
for my power is made perfect in weakness." …
2 Corinthians 12:9

Several weeks after I was diagnosed with Parkinson's, our pastor asked us to thank God for something He had given us in our life. Immediately, I thanked God for giving me Parkinson's. I thanked Him because this disease was making me more dependent on Him and showing me I was not as self-sufficient as I thought I was. It was easy for me, a man who had a relatively easy life, to think I was in control. Parkinson's helped me understand that God ordained my path and I must depend on Him. It had drawn me closer to God as my Father and closer to His Word as my guide on this journey. It helped me see what is important in life. Parkinson's made me view Romans 8:38–39 as a promise of eternal love given to me by Almighty God. This scripture says, *I am convinced that neither death nor life, neither angels nor demons, neither the present nor the future, nor any powers, neither height nor depth, nor anything else in all creation, will be able to separate us from the love of God that is in Christ Jesus our Lord.* My prayer was, and still is, "Lord Jesus, thank You for saving me, a sinner; cleanse me, change me, guide me, and deepen me. I love You."

On October 28, 2005, we had an in-service day at school. I saw Suzanne Fischer, a dear friend who had been a student teacher in my classroom in the fall of 1990. I told her about Parkinson's. She expressed her concern and love, and then she asked, "Why, Rick, oh, why you? You are a man of faith. God will get you through this." The statement that I was a man of faith was spoken at the wrong time for me. It came just when my speeding roller coaster car flew over the top of the highest hill and I sped down and went into a loop. At the top of the loop, the car stopped and I was hanging upside down. As I hung there, I silently wished I really was the man of faith some people think I am. There are some days when I doubt God, I question God, and I second-guess God. This day was one of those days. While hanging upside down, I began to realize my thinking was as upside down as my body.

When I got home, I told Terri how I had been frustrated all day. I hadn't done anything other than sit and listen to a speaker all morning, eat a catered lunch, and work in a small group for an hour in the afternoon. I was extremely tired at the end of the day. I hated it. Terri said it would take a while to accept the changes in my life, that I couldn't and wouldn't accept them overnight. When we went to bed, she snored, so I went downstairs. I cried, even more frustrated than I was earlier in the day. As my mind slowly turned off, I remembered the words to this old hymn:

> O soul, are you weary and troubled?
> No light in the darkness you see?
> There's light for a look at the Savior,
> And life more abundant and free.
>
> Turn your eyes upon Jesus,
> Look full in His wonderful face,
> And the things of earth will grow strangely dim,
> In the light of His glory and grace.[1]

I was determined to look to him when I couldn't sleep. This sounded good for that day, but could I make it a part of my thinking for every day?

---

[1]   Helen H. Lemmel, "Turn Your Eyes Upon Jesus" (public domain).

When school resumed the next day, I was concerned that my frustration with the symptoms of Parkinson's and my lack of patience would spill over into my classroom. I knew the atmosphere in my classroom was a major factor in how well my students behaved and how much they learned. I prayed, "Lord, help me to be patient, to react as You would, and to build up and not tear down my students, even when I don't feel good. Help me to let my relationship with Christ soak into my relationships with my students."

I read 2 Corinthians 12:9, *But he said to me, "My grace is sufficient for you, for my power is made perfect in weakness." Therefore I will boast all the more gladly about my weaknesses, so that Christ's power may rest on me.* I said to the Lord, "I don't understand this. How is there power in weakness? Will Your power only be on me if I am weak? How does this apply to Parkinson's? Am I so bullheaded I need to be taught through a chronic illness?"

I listened for an answer, but God was silent. I wasn't used to talking to God and not getting an answer. This made me think the worst, and I began to focus on the negatives as I tried to talk to God. With bitterness in my heart, I said, "I'm down emotionally. I'm depressed. My progress has leveled out after being diagnosed for only four months. Is this as good as I'm going to get? I didn't sign up for this. God, where are You hiding?"

As I was questioning God, I realized I had climbed back on the roller coaster ride. My desire had been to get off of it and let it just go away. What I needed was something positive to replace those negatives. It happened one month later, when I went to see my doctor.

I saw Dr. Alberto Espay, a neurologist who specializes in movement disorders. He was very upbeat. He said I was really responding well to the medicine. The results of his tests (small motor skills, walking, cognitive skills, and balance tests) showed I had about a fifty-percent improvement in these areas. He thought I could respond even more positively with an increase in the medicine I was taking. As I was leaving, he came down the hall and said he had forgotten to give me the results from my MRI.

He laughed and said, "The results were very positive. They show that you really do have a brain." Seeing him was encouraging and I prayed simply, "Lord, thank You that there are good doctors, effective medicines, and continued research into this disease." This visit and the great attitude of my doctor took me off the emotion-filled roller coaster. But, could I stay off?

The next day, I told my students about Parkinson's because I had to take medicine during the day. Once again, verbally saying it was hard because it made it seem so real. There was no denying that I had a chronic illness. Who would have thought this would happen to me? And so I prayed, "Lord, I don't believe You give us more than we can handle. Please help me get off this emotional roller coaster and help me handle this Your way. I am asking You to extend Your gift of grace to my aching heart."

GRACE

Chapter 4

The Highest Hill, The Longest Drop

Even in laughter the heart may ache,
and rejoicing may end in grief.
Proverbs 14:13

A person's steps are directed by the LORD.
How then can anyone understand their own way?
Proverbs 20:24

After being diagnosed with Parkinson's disease in 2005, I continued teaching for the next three years. The first year, I missed four days of teaching and the second year, I missed seven days. I was in good shape at the start of the third year.

In July 2007, I went on a weeklong fishing trip with my son Philip and four friends. We went to Boundary Waters, a lake-filled wilderness area in northern Minnesota, accessible only by canoe. Everything we needed to set up a campsite had to be carried in. Our time there was spent relaxing, fishing, canoeing, and hiking. We blazed our own trail around two nearby lakes. We caught about sixty good-sized fish, and every evening some of them became our main dish for dinner. Each day included sitting on a cliff above our campsite, talking and teasing each other.

The trip was great, and the fishing was way beyond my expectations. I was well-rested, had a great tan, looked fit, and felt pretty good. I knew I could conquer the world. I was ready to get back into the swing of things, totally unaware my roller coaster car had just climbed to the top of the highest hill, and it was about to make the fastest and scariest descent that I had ever experienced.

This descent began when Terri and I spent the night at Phill and Rita's house in Indianapolis. We had spent the Labor Day weekend helping them prepare for the wedding and reception for their youngest daughter. It was a long, stressful weekend, which ended with a massive cleanup. When we got back to their house around midnight on Saturday evening, we were exhausted, and had no trouble falling asleep.

Around 1:30 a.m., Terri woke up and went to the bathroom. As she returned to her room, she misjudged where her door was and fell down the stairs. I woke up to what sounded like the whole house was caving in and rushed to the bottom of the stairway. Her head was bleeding and two fingers on her left hand were bent back toward her wrist. Phill and Rita helped her off the steps and cleaned the blood off her head and neck. They thought she had two broken fingers and the cut on her head needed some stitches. We wondered if she had a concussion, so we took her to the emergency room at a nearby hospital.

Terri's injuries were treated there. She did not have a concussion. She had a scratch on her head that bled a lot, but did not require stitches, a broken finger on her left hand, and a hematoma on her left calf. Considering the fall she had taken, she was hardly injured at all. The Lord had protected her from serious injury.

After Terri was taken care of, we had a steady stream of hospital staff come in and talk to us. There were three nurses, two doctors, and a social worker, who asked us about our marriage and about our relationship with each other. They were trying to determine if I was physically abusing Terri. It was a very stressful situation. Although Terri ended up with just three minor injuries, this whole incident took a physical and emotional toll on me. We had been awake all night at the hospital. I had only had an hour and a half of sleep in two days. We had a two-hour-and-fifteen-minute drive to get home. This was a recipe for a disaster.

The next day I was exhausted, but I returned to teaching. This exhaustion, along with the stress of dealing with the symptoms of Parkinson's disease, made the downhill plunge seem like it was totally out of control. It carried over into every aspect of my life. I had the worst fatigue I could imagine, and I could teach only four days a week. I took off almost every Friday. The first three quarters of school, I missed twenty-five days, which was almost a day each week.

I noticed many of my symptoms were returning. I started having facial tremors, my gait became slow, and I was losing my fine motor skills. I had no energy when I had extra work at school or when working around the house. My back, shoulders, and neck became very stiff. My roller coaster car was going downhill fast.

On March 11, 2008, at 1:30 a.m., I went into my son Philip's room to ask him to turn down his radio. As I turned to leave, I passed out. My back was against the door, so Terri could not get the door open to get to me. Philip finally pulled me away from the door, Terri rushed in, and they got me back to bed. I agreed not to get out of bed unless Terri or Philip was with me. We thanked the Lord for protecting me from any serious injury when I passed out. What a gift!

The next day I saw Dr. Bort, my primary care physician. He said I had a concussion. My blood pressure was 112/96 lying down, 98/70 sitting, and 90/64 while standing. He thought I had orthostatic hypotension. He wanted me to increase my water and salt intake, and begin wearing compression stockings.

The roller coaster was picking up speed at a dangerous rate and seemed to be jumping off the track. I was scared. I began to realize I wouldn't be able to teach next year. I hoped and prayed that if I followed my doctor's orders, I could finish the last ten weeks of school.

Instead, my symptoms worsened, so I began to pray that the Lord would show me what to do. On Sunday, March 16, 2007, I believe God impressed on my heart that I should retire at the end of the school year. On Wednesday, March 19, I told the principal I would be retiring in June. The district personnel director told me I could use all my sick days if I had a note from my doctor stating that I wasn't able to teach. I taught four days that week and I was wiped out. I didn't know it then, but those four days were the last days I would ever teach.

The next week was spring break. On Friday, March 26, I returned to the doctor. My blood pressure was lower than it had been before. It was 90/64 while sitting and 78/48 while standing. Dr. Bort and Dr. Espay talked, and they decided to put me on Midodrine to stabilize my blood pressure. The medicine took several days to begin working. Terri was monitoring my blood pressure at home, and sometimes it was so low she could not even hear the bottom number (60/? or 65/38). As we considered the impact of my low blood pressure, we knew it was too risky for me to continue to teach; my teaching career was over.

This realization made me feel like I was trapped on a runaway roller coaster which was plunging downhill at a dangerous speed. I wondered if and when I could get off. I asked myself if I would be able to endure the ups and downs, the steep hills, and the dangerous curves I would have to go through.

"Oh, God! Where are You?"

PROTECTION

Chapter 5

Hearing The Snow Fall

The heavens declare the glory of God;
the skies proclaim the work of his hands.
Psalm 19:1

When my glory passes by,
I will put you in a cleft in the rock
and cover you with my hand
until I have passed by.
Exodus 33:22

Little did I know that the Lord, early in my disease, had already given me the way off the roller coaster. My son Philip and I had gone hunting on a friend's property in December 2005. As I sat in my deer stand that cold morning, God sharpened my eyesight and my hearing, and taught me a valuable lesson. I captured it all in a poem at that time. Recalling the poem is what helped me off the scary roller coaster ride.

Hearing the Snow Fall; I Will Cover You

Stepping from the light of the hunting trailer,

The morning air feels cold and deep.

The wind slaps me in the face,

And my breath freezes as it escapes from my mouth.

The darkness swallows the light from my small flashlight
As I slowly walk the trail that leads to my tree stand.
Leaving this familiar path that follows the top of the ridge,
My feet cause the leaves underfoot to crackle.

I step on a twig and it breaks,
The sound seems to carry to the other side of the woods.
As I push an ice covered branch out of my way,
The layer of ice splinters and falls to the ground.

I climb into my deer stand and attach my safety harness.
I settle in and begin to listen to the sounds of the awakening forest.
As dawn breaks, chipmunks scurry through the leaves,
Jump across a fallen tree, and disappear into a hole in a rotting log.

Squirrels pursue each other from one tree to another,
Stopping only to chatter loudly, and then renew the chase.
A woodpecker flies in behind me and lands on a shagbark hickory.
He begins to peck and the hammering rings through the woods.

Two crows appear overhead,
Cawing loudly and chasing each other through the trees.
I look for the deer path that runs beneath my stand
And I can see hoofprints in the damp soil.

As the dim dawn light climbs over the hill,
I spot a turkey rub just a few feet from my stand.
I then notice there are seven other rubs,
Telling me that a flock of turkeys has been looking for food.

Slowly and gently, as the forest awakens around me,
I drift off into a very light sleep.
I awaken as I feel dampness on my cheek;
I notice instantly that the woods are filled with a faint pitter-
    pattering sound.

There is a light snow falling on the leaves on the forest floor.
As it hits, each flake makes a small, very faint sound.
I listen intently, and notice that the snow
Makes a slightly different sound as it hits my jeans.

I watch and listen as the snow lands on my boots and then melts.
Now, I listen to another slightly louder and even more distinct
    sound
As the snow settles on my orange hunting jacket and then slowly
    slides off.
I sit in wonder, listening to sounds I've never noticed or
    experienced before.

Suddenly, I see movement just to my left.
A young doe seems to materialize right before my eyes.
She's just twenty-five feet from me
But she doesn't see me.

She cautiously walks along the path;
She finds some tender shoots and she begins to graze on them.
She sniffs the air and a patch of ground under a pine tree.
Surprisingly, she lays down on this soft bed of pine needles.

I don't move, afraid I'll spook her,

And spoil the moment.

I watch her and admire her beauty,

Noticing that the snow is falling on her coat and not melting.

Slowly and softly, the snow covers her body.

I sit in awe and say to myself, "Be still."

As I take in the splendor of the forest being covered in a blanket of white snow,

I feel strongly that I am sitting in a holy place.

In the stillness and beauty of the moment, God's Spirit whispers to me,

"Rick, just as you've watched Me cover My creation with a white blanket of snow,

So, I too, will cover you with the gifts of My love and peace.

Trust Me.

I know you have Parkinson's disease.

I gave it to you.

It is a gift that will teach you to trust and depend on Me.

Again, I will cover you as I transform you into the man I want you to be."

Suddenly, the wind shifts and the doe smells me.

She immediately springs to her feet and bounds away.

I just sit in wonder and amazement;

And I pray, "Lord, cover me."

I have read this poem several times each year since I've been diagnosed with Parkinson's. It has always brought me back to the promises of God. That day, the Lord used the wonder of His creation to assure me He would cover me with His love and peace as He guided me on the adventure ahead. I've needed this reminder as I continue to learn what it takes to live with God's gift of Parkinson's disease.

COVERING LOVE
AND PEACE

PART 2

A LITTLE HOPE TO OVERFLOWING HOPE

CHAPTERS 6–10

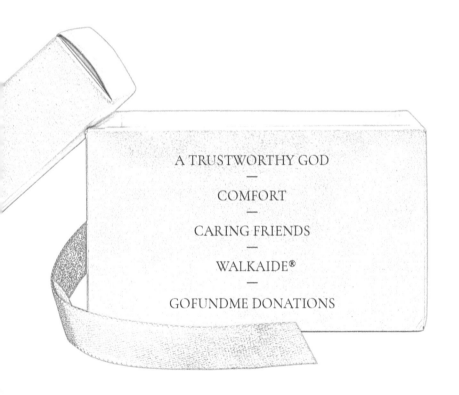

A TRUSTWORTHY GOD
—
COMFORT
—
CARING FRIENDS
—
WALKAIDE®
—
GOFUNDME DONATIONS

Chapter 6
Retired and Replaced

… "What no eye has seen,
what no ear has heard,
and what no human mind has conceived"—
the things God
has prepared for those who love him—
these are the things
God has revealed to us by his Spirit.
1 Corinthians 2:9–10

On Saturday, March 27, 2007, after much prayer and talking with Terri and Philip, we decided I would retire from teaching the following Monday. With my symptoms getting worse, more medicines being prescribed, having low blood pressure, and passing out at home, we were certain this was the right decision. I called my principal and told her. We had discussed this several times in the past two months, so she was not surprised. Monday was an in-service day, and she agreed to let me tell the faculty then. I knew it would be an emotional time, so I wrote a letter.

On Monday, I read my letter aloud.

* * *

The first day of school, I told the other third-grade teachers, Sharon, Kim, and Danielle, I was very apprehensive about this school year. I didn't know what would happen with my Parkinson's disease, and I didn't know if I'd make it through the year. I know now that I won't make it through this year. I have felt pretty bad three of the past five weeks. Many of you don't know that on March 11, I passed out at home and had a concussion. I spent three days of spring break at the doctor's office and in the hospital, having several tests done, to hopefully find out why my blood pressure was so erratic. My blood pressure bottomed out at 78/48 (average is 120/80). I'm very light-headed and I'm not driving. I don't want anything to happen here at school in front of the students. That would be hard on them and on me.

So today is my last day. I'll be around to clean up my room, encourage students at RAT and MAT time. I'll come back for track-and-field day and on the last day of school. This will give me closure.

In third grade we've teased all year that Sharon is my mother, Kim my trophy wife (after losing Lez, who was my school wife for 27 years), and Danielle is my daughter. I want to say publicly they really were my wonderful family this year. They carried me more than you will ever know. I want to say thank you to them. They have been great to work with. For the rest of you, thank you for praying for me, helping me, and encouraging me.

May I share my heart? Terri and I have discussed retirement for about six months. The week of spring break we decided I would retire at the end of the school year. This week was Holy Week. As I thought about retirement, I also thought about what I believe about Holy Week. I really believe what Jesus Christ went through that week was for me. He died and rose again for my soul. I really believe this and trust in it. I've had this thought: If I am trusting Jesus Christ with my soul, why can't I trust Him with my life? And so I do.

Today, a new chapter in my life begins. Where will it take me? Who knows? God does, and I choose to trust

Him. Before I sit down I'd like to say just a short prayer: Heavenly Father, thank you for friends who love me. May You bless them and their families richly. I trust You and I love You. Amen.

* * *

After reading this letter, I left the meeting and went downstairs to my room to get lesson plans together for the substitute teacher. And then it hit me: there wasn't going to be a substitute teacher! The principal would be hiring someone to take my place.

As I was thinking about this and collecting materials, there was a knock on my door. A young woman introduced herself and told me she had been hired to take my place. Unthinkable! I looked at the clock. I had been replaced in just two hours. That was a very humbling experience. I felt like I was being robbed of a large portion of my identity. After all, in my neck of the woods, I was known as Mr. Iles, The Science Guy, and I was respected as a third-grade science and math teacher. Now, who was I?

I knew God would use the events that had happened in the past three years to begin a new chapter in my life. I prayed, "Lord, right now I feel like Parkinson's is my foe and I really don't like it. Help me to think Your thoughts as I internalize the fact that my teaching days are over. I believe as I begin this new phase in my life, You will reveal to me how You will make this disease my friend. You told me Parkinson's was a gift You chose to give to me. I'm trusting You to do what You have determined is best for me and for Your Kingdom. My experiences have always shown just how trustworthy You really are. Right now I'm trying to understand this verse of Scripture, *No eye has seen, no ear has heard, no mind has conceived, what God has prepared for those who love him* (1 Corinthians 2:9). I'm anxious to know what You have prepared for me.

Thank You for the gift of Parkinson's disease and for the gift of trust. Thank You for allowing me to share my heart with You. I'm asking 'Why?' with a humble heart and not a clenched fist. Please change me, cleanse me, guide me, and deepen me into the person You want me to be, and use me for Your purposes. I'm asking in the name of Jesus. Amen."

A TRUSTWORTHY
GOD

Chapter 7

What's to Celebrate?

Many are the plans in a person's heart,
but it is the LORD's purpose that prevails.
Proverbs 19:21

I had retired from teaching ten weeks before the end of the school year, but I still thought of the students as "my" class. I went to see them three times during those ten weeks. I encouraged them to do their best on the state tests, cheered for them on track-and-field day, and told them goodbye on the last day of school.

Time began to speed up after the school year ended. Vacations, swimming, going to camp, and playing outside all day seemed to make time fly by. August came too soon, and summer's carefree days were now memories. It was time to return to school. I had experienced the routine of this passing of time for thirty-one years. But this year was different; I wasn't going back to my classroom. My teaching days were over, and I wasn't handling this realization too well. I felt useless and wondered what I would do with my time.

Five friends invited me to go out to lunch: Lez, Cindy, Viv, Sharon, and Peggy. All of them had retired in the last two years. They asked me to join them even though I was on sick leave and not officially retired. They wanted to celebrate their retirement, and they wanted to tease Kim McCoy and some other friends who were still working. All of them could celebrate. They retired because they wanted to. But I wasn't in a celebratory mood and didn't want to go out with them. I didn't feel the same way they did about retirement. At age fifty-six I wasn't mentally ready for this stage of life. I decided I would stay home and pout. While my friends were celebrating, I was going to have a pity party with myself. Just the two of us. Two voices in my head. Rick and Mr. Iles. We had quite a conversation.

Rick: We have been robbed!

Mr. Iles: What are you talking about?

Rick: We were forced out of teaching by Parkinson's disease. Forced out! We were robbed! Thank you, Parkinson's.

Mr. Iles: I don't feel robbed. Think about how healthy we were for the first fifty years of our life. Instead of saying, "Thank you, Parkinson's," we need to say, "Thank You, Lord."

Rick: I guess you are going to tell me how lucky we were to save up 262 days of sick leave.

Mr. Iles: Not lucky, but blessed.

Rick: So what! We are still out. Low blood pressure and other symptoms of Parkinson's disease forced us out.

Mr. Iles: Don't focus on being forced out. Remember how successful we were in the classroom. The year before we retired, we received an award from the Hamilton County Board of Education and another award from the Delshire PTA for excellence in teaching. We went out on top and so did our students. Ninety percent of them passed the State Test in mathematics.

Rick: Big deal. We still were forced out and we lost our identity.

Mr. Iles: You're crazy. We did not lose our identity. God began changing it and I don't think He is finished working on us.

Rick: Well, I don't like any change. Maybe God is wasting our talents.

Mr. Iles: A waste of talent? We taught for thirty-one years and it was not a waste.

Rick: You won't change my mind. It was a waste!

Mr. Iles: I suppose you thought we were indispensable. I'd like to remind you that we were replaced in two hours. Do you remember how we felt?

Rick: Yes, we couldn't believe it and we were humbled. We asked why any of this had to happen. We still had a lot to give.

Mr. Iles: Yes, we did, but at what price? Having a new curriculum and working with three new teachers would have stressed us out. Forced retirement spared us from experiencing those changes.

Rick: Speaking of change, let's change the subject. This stinking disease makes us one-half the man we used to be. We hate it. We work in slow motion, our thinking isn't clear, we are emotional and cry often, we are off-balance, and sometimes we fall. We force ourself to eat. We have extreme fatigue and we try to stay up until 9:00 p.m. every evening. Sometimes we don't make it past 7:00 p.m. It seems as if we are always trying to catch up.

Mr. Iles: Wow! Aren't we negative tonight? How about being thankful?

Rick: Thankful for what?

Mr. Iles: Our medicines are working well and our overall health is better than when we retired. Dr. Espay says we have the best kind of Parkinson's disease. Our worst day is better than some patients' best day.

Rick: Do you think our worst day is good?

Mr. Iles: That is not what I said.

Rick: I know what you said, and I think you are as nutty as a fruitcake. It's crazy to think bad days lead to opportunities for growth.

Mr. Iles: You should know, since you are as nutty as me. After all, we do share the same body.

Rick: Back to our best and our worst. On our best days, it is not too hard to see what God is using to shape us, but on our worst days, we still struggle with the methods He uses to chisel us. How in the world did He decide that adversities can be turned into opportunities? Sometimes I think there has to be a better way.

Mr. Iles: Don't forget what God says: *All things work together for good to those who love him and are called according to his purpose* (Romans 8:28). Come on! Let's get it together and put our trust in Him. This pity party is officially over!

* * *

The next morning I was awake at 2:00 a.m. and the negatives outweighed the positives. I prayed, "Lord, please don't allow Satan to use this against me. I just need to share my heart. Give me comfort. I really never expected to feel this way. I guess I've kept it all on the back burner and now that it is time for school to begin, I really am feeling out of sorts because I'm not going to work. Who would have thought at age fifty-six, I would be disabled and not able to teach? Please don't allow me to hop back on the roller coaster ride. I don't think I could handle it right now."

God heard my prayer, and He impressed on my heart that He listens and cares, He protects and comforts. He reminded me He is big enough to hear even my complaints. Even in the midst of these complaints, as I interacted with the Lord, He graciously and gradually gave me the gift of trust. "Thank You, Lord."

COMFORT

Chapter 8

He Saw Me Walking

… they will walk and not be faint.
Isaiah 40:31

A small group in our church, led by Rick Frank, sponsored an annual music festival in the city of Dayton, Kentucky. Rick recruited workers for a carnival for the children who would attend. Terri and I were working in the prize tent. I was socializing with kids and their parents, as well as greeting and talking to friends working at the festival. I was doing a lot of walking, and was having a hard time just crossing the field. I didn't know it at the time, but Rob Pinkston, a certified prosthetist whom I met at church, was watching me. He saw me walking. He noticed that each step was painful for me.

Around 3:00 p.m., Rob brought his kids into the prize tent so they could turn in their game cards and select their prizes. After chatting for a couple of minutes, he asked if I had a few minutes to go outside and talk. He said he had wanted to talk to me for about a month, but didn't know if he should. This really sparked my interest. When I asked him what it was about, his reply surprised me. He wanted to know about my Parkinson's and why I limped so badly. He noticed earlier that I shuffled when I walked and didn't lift my left foot. He could tell each step was painful. He asked about my symptoms, and I told him about having tremors, extreme fatigue, dyskinesia, cognitive issues, and loss of strength. I told him I had dystonia in my left foot and it was always cramped. He asked how it was being treated. I told him I was getting Botox shots, which were very painful and only masked the pain without solving the problem.

Rob told me he had a device, called a WalkAide®, that I might be able to use to get rid of the cramping. If it worked, I might even be able to walk normally again. He told me to set up an appointment with his office manager and we would try it out. Before we left, I asked him why he didn't want to tell me about the WalkAide®. He said he didn't want to get my hopes up and have those hopes shattered if it didn't work. Also, for my diagnosis, use of the WalkAide® was off-label, and therefore, my insurance would probably not help with the cost. However, after seeing me walk, he decided it was worth these risks.

When I arrived at his office, Rob described the WalkAide® as an electrical stimulation device that sends impulses to your foot and ankle. It's a small computer strapped to your leg. He explained that Parkinson's disease had stolen the connection between my knee and my ankle, and my nerves were not getting the messages from my brain down to my foot. This device should restore that stolen connection. He coordinated it with a computer, did some tests, entered something into the computer, and turned it on. It worked immediately. It took the cramping away, and it told my foot how high to lift, how far to extend for my stride, and even how to hit the ground. Rob and I were both elated!

Rob let me use his WalkAide® on trial for two months. He even let me take it on vacation. Having it was wonderful. I felt normal again. Since I didn't have the awful pain in my foot, and I was not having severe pain elsewhere, I had the energy to do things I had not done in several months. I could walk without pain. I could climb stairs without having to put both feet on each step. I could play basketball and other sports again. I could take a walk with my wife and keep up with her. It literally changed my life.

After returning from vacation, Terri and I discussed purchasing the WalkAide®. Rob offered to sell it to us at his cost, which was $6,000. He agreed to let us pay it off slowly, at $50 a month. We decided to buy the WalkAide®, even if we had to take ten years to pay it off.

A short time later, I went to a wedding where I saw Charlie Fehrman, the co-director of the summer camp where I ministered. He saw me walking and he told me I looked better than I had looked in a long time. He knew something was different, but couldn't pin it down. I told him about the WalkAide®. He then asked me about the cost, and I told him it was $6,000 and my insurance company would not cover it.

Sometime in the next few days, he discussed this with his family and they started a *GoFundMe* account to pay for my WalkAide®. They emailed everyone they knew and contacted their friends on Facebook and on other social media to get the word out. In the first three days of the fundraiser, they collected over $6,000. At the end of the thirty-one days, they had raised $13,087.70. By some miracle, all of this happened without me knowing about it.

I was totally surprised when my doorbell rang on Thanksgiving morning 2014 and I found Charlie Fehrman on my doorstep. My family was eager for me to let him in because they knew what was happening. I asked, "What are you doing here?" I still didn't have a clue. Charlie showed me the video of his appeal for donations and then handed me a check for $13,087.70. I just cried. I had no words to express my gratitude. I still cry when I tell this story. It

Unbelievable! $13,087.70! I think I'll cry.

was a terrific day in the Iles household.

But the story wasn't over yet. On Tuesday of the next week, I went to Rob's office to pay off the WalkAide®. We watched the *GoFundMe* video and laughed and cried together. He asked his office manager how much I owed and she replied $5,300.70. I remembered there were seventy cents in the check that I was given. It seemed strange to me at that time, but now it made sense. God is certainly a God of details.

This money not only paid for the WalkAide®, but it allowed us to build a much-needed bathroom for me on the first floor of our home. There was even some money left over. I asked one donor's permission to give his portion to another Parkinson's patient. He agreed and we helped a young man pay for his WalkAide®. God is good, all the time.

Not only was I blessed by what the WalkAide® itself did for me, I was also overwhelmed by the amount of money that was donated to me. Indeed, the Lord has given me wonderful friends. He is a great God who answers prayers. Perhaps my mother said it best: "If God wants you to have the WalkAide®, then he will provide a way for you to get it." And He did!!

"Lord, thank You for the gift of caring friends, especially Rob and Charlie. The opportunity to experience the blessing of giving was also a gift you gave my many friends. And finally, thank You for the gift of the WalkAide®."

CARING
FRIENDS

Chapter 9

The WalkAide®

by Rob Pinkston,
certified prosthetist and close friend

Give, and it will be given to you …
Luke 6:38

I met Rick when he began attending Highland Hills Church. We were in the same Bible study group for several weeks. I was surprised when I learned he had been diagnosed with Parkinson's disease. He did not have some of the most common symptoms of this disease. He did not have resting tremors, impaired balance issues, and no noticeable cognitive issues. I thought all Parkinson's patients had these symptoms. However, he had two other symptoms which were very painful; drop foot and dystonia in his left foot. While talking to him, I realized he was struggling to understand and internalize some of the information he had recently learned about these two symptoms. He was wondering if there were any medicines or treatments that would help him overcome the pain in his left foot. I knew it was very likely his drop foot and dystonia were both a result of Parkinson's disease. But I also knew the technology of a device named a WalkAide®, and I believed it was physically possible for this device to stimulate the muscles in Rick's ankle and foot, and I thought this could be very beneficial for him.

So, what is a WalkAide®? It is a small electrical device

that functions as a neuroprosthesis, medically referred to as a functional electrical stimulator. It is about the size of a flip phone that suspends in a cuff just below the knee. A tilt sensor and accelerometer in the WalkAide® read its relationship to the floor, measuring any angular change or speed change that occurs in any direction. After a program is set to the users' personal parameters, the WalkAide® will send a signal directly to the muscle via a set of sticky-backed electrodes. This signal tells the foot when to lift, how high to lift, how far to stride, and how to touch the ground. During the swing phase of walking, the WalkAide® electrically stimulates the nerve that is just below the knee. This activates the muscle that raises the foot as it signals the ankle to dorsiflex. The WalkAide® runs on a single AA battery that needs to be changed every month. When the electrodes are well maintained, they need to be changed every two weeks to a month.

Knowing the potential of the WalkAide®, I thought it was worth a try for Rick. Personally, if I didn't tell Rick about it because of my fear that it might not work, I would have second-guessed that decision every time I saw him struggling to walk. So when I saw him at the park, I decided to talk to him about it.

I explained that if the WalkAide® worked, it could improve his walking ability. His gait would be faster, smoother, more natural, and he would have a safer stepping motion. These improvements could result in longer distances covered, increased mobility, functionality, and overall independence. The WalkAide® had the potential to re-engage Rick's existing nerve pathways and muscles. This recruitment of existing muscles could result in reduction of atrophy and fatigue. It could improve circulation, improve voluntary control, and increase joint range of motion. I've seen many patients try it with exceptional results. I believed Rick would have this same success, so I invited him to come to my office and check it out.

The WalkAide® worked immediately for Rick. We were elated and thrilled. I let him use the WalkAide® on a trial basis for the next two months, and then many of Rick's friends and family donated money to a *GoFundMe* account to pay for the WalkAide®.

Rick is truly a blessed man.

A few months later, another friend, Gary, challenged Rick to train for a year and then run a 5K fundraising race. Rick accepted the challenge and started his training. He set a goal of running the race between thirty and forty minutes. Gary and I thought this was a lofty goal and wondered if he could do it.

I ran the race with Rick. I was pretty blown away seeing a guy who could barely walk a few months ago, running at such a fast and smooth pace. It was unreal to see him run. We finished the course with a time of 31:36. It was amazing and very humbling to run with Rick that day. My knees may not have been quite as happy to be in the race, but that's a different story.

Rick told me I was very gracious to him. I don't know exactly what he meant by that. Hopefully, I treated him with the same kindness I know he would have extended to me if I were in his shoes. I know he has a heart to help people. I know he has a heart to want what is best for his friends. He and I are no different in that respect. There are costs associated with providing technology like the WalkAide®, and Rick had an awful lot of friends willing to help him afford this cool technology. If anyone was gracious, he and I both know it's the good Lord above. He put us together in situations orchestrated by Him so we could know one another and become friends. My heart was filled with joy in a humble sense of gratefulness, knowing that God blessed Rick with a miracle, and He allowed this cool technology to work for Rick, even when science said it shouldn't.

I think Rick is an amazing guy and a humble servant of the Lord. I've learned a lot about patience and perseverance while watching him from afar. I've been in his home and seen the things he holds dear. I've listened to him encourage others at church, and I've heard him share his faith in public. I'm proud to be his friend. I want to thank him for being willing to try something outside of the box that potentially could help somebody else. It has been a joy to watch from the sidelines and see my friend experiencing the benefits of this special device. What a gift! God is good.

Chapter 10

GoFundMe and "RetireTheCane"

by Charlie Fehrman,
co–director of Camp Chazon and close friend

A generous person will prosper;
whoever refreshes others will be refreshed.
Proverbs 11:25

My friend Rick Iles has always been eternally young. From the days when he had a car and a girlfriend (and I had neither), he always looked younger. As we grew into our thirties and forties, he continued to look younger. Always the baby-face. Always tireless. Always athletic.

He and I served together in a summer camp youth program since our teenage days, growing into co-director roles, and we literally lived together during the heat of each summer, with no AC and with the weight of caring for 150-plus kids, begging for fun, attention, and direction. Those were some of the best days of our lives, laced with fun, tears, difficulties, and so much joy. The two-way-street kind of joy, in which you receive more than you give. With endless days of softball, kickball, trail hikes, and simply walking to everything, there was no lack of steps and exercise. In spite of all that required movement, Rick would find time each day to go run. We tried logic, we tried shaming, we tried interventions—but he would run. So, I guess it's easy to deduce that running was important to him.

One morning at that summer camp, Rick told me that he just didn't feel right. He tried to tough it out, but "it" was not a twenty-four-hour bug. Being late in the camping year and with an easy crowd, I encouraged Rick to go home, rest up, and get well.

Neither he nor I knew it would be the last time he would be at that camp.

* * *

Parkinson's is a silent and particularly cruel enemy. It is worse than a disease—it steals and never gives back. It steals different things from different victims, which adds to its insidiousness and difficulty to predict. It stole a lot from my friend Rick—but listen long enough to him and he'll convince you that it gave to him as well.

* * *

It took a few weeks for word to reach back to the sleepy hills of Indiana where the summer camp was. Rick was sick. Really sick. Now, the always baby-faced, always tireless, always athletic man I knew was … always different. Every time I saw him, Parkinson's had taken a little more. He walked beside me in my own chapter of grief a few times, so I didn't have the awkwardness of not knowing what to say—I just had the pain of seeing my friend change monthly.

Trials, experimental drugs, and blind studies all became his staples in life. The closest Rick had ever gotten to the medical community was marrying a nurse—but now he was on a first-name acquaintance with one of the most-renowned physicians in the world. Not a perk whose dues any of us would gladly pay. There were conversations about surgeries and non-approved treatments, there were late night internet searches for topics we had never heard of before, but in which we were slowly becoming adroit. Again, *not* how one plans to spend their weekend, let alone the rest of their life.

In a random (or predestined) effort, a doctor prescribed a device off-label for Rick that strapped to his leg. He had developed a lazy foot—not the scientific term, but the realistic one. His foot and knee couldn't coordinate their movements together and Rick not only was in pain and at a high fall risk, but he could barely walk. This electronic device, while not meant for his situation, changed his life—in the first positive way in a while. It generated electronic impulses when his knee moved and those pulses "woke up" his ankle so that it could move. He could walk. And in a few weeks of tweaking location and amperage, he even had hopes he could run again. Hope is a key ingredient to fighting any foe, but especially ones as personal as Parkinson's. This little device—a WalkAide®—gave Rick hope that he hadn't had in a long time. He would call to report his progress and we'd laugh and sometimes cry together.

* * *

Rick has spent his whole life as a teacher of elementary children. He considers it his calling—and he should. Rave reviews abound about "Mr. Iles' classrooms and field trips." His wife chose to stay at home and raise their kids—and they were the quintessential family. Frugal to a fault, as self-sufficient as they were generous. So, when Rick called me that evening, I just assumed it was another update on a newly-found benefit of his WalkAide®. Instead, he led with this sentence, "The insurance won't pay for my WalkAide®." It was like a stab in the heart to me, and worse for Rick. It was just bad news to me about my friend—but it was stripping away hope for him. I've never been one to just accept bad news on its face. There has to be an angle, a misunderstanding, an appeal—so my bull-in-a-china-shop mind kicked in and I was firing questions, and "They can't do that" in the best intentions, but it wasn't producing any change within Rick. He was just defeated and it was a terrible thing to experience— even on the phone.

* * *

Within a couple of weeks of that conversation, I had a challenge of my own I had been planning. We were closing down a ministry I had been part of from the beginning, and I wanted to close it down with honor, integrity, and celebration. On the final day of the public ministry, my kids had come in from the four corners of the world to support me and share that day. Add to that, an uncanny number of faces from those summer camp days showed up, too. I was surprised, humbled, and blessed. It helped salve the bruises of that day for me, to be sure. After all the hugging and thank yous and good-byes were finished, this close-knit group of family and friends was lingering on my back deck, laughing over stories of childhood antics. I knew Rick would have reveled in that scene as much as I did.

With no plan or even a good transition, I just blurted out what Rick was going through and what his latest bad news was. "It just didn't seem right to me," I said, "that the eternally young and vibrant Rick Iles should be using a cane to meagerly get around." And somehow, though I don't remember the phrasing or lead up, the phrase "Retire the cane" started being repeated.

Like a pack of dogs with fresh meat, this group of twenty-somethings began to brainstorm and divide and conquer. All I needed was a white board to feel like I was back in my element. Then, one of them who is gifted in videography, started moving chairs around and pulled out his ubiquitous iPhone. He moved me over to a certain chair and said, "Tell that story again like none of us know Rick." And in that group of amazing "kids," the *GoFundMe* account to "RetireTheCane" was born.

I've never been more proud to have influenced a group of people, nor to be associated with them now as a peer. We set our goal for the $6,000 necessary to purchase a new WalkAide®, and threw in that Rick's home only had an upstairs bathroom, and that it would be an amazing gift to be able to put a bathroom on the main level of his home.

That started on September 7, 2014, and by November 15, we had received $13,087.70. Eighty percent of the gifts were given by people who had wandered through that summer camp over the years, and most of the gifts were under $200.

Rick knew nothing about any of this, so on Thanksgiving Day, it was with a look of shock that Rick opened the door to let my brood into his home. Never one to stand on ceremony, he asked, "What are you doing here?" I told him that we wanted to share a video with him if he could get his family on the couch to watch it, and then we'd be on our way. His family gathered on the couch trying to feign bewilderment—though they all knew ahead of time and were eager to watch their dad's face when he realized what was happening. They had known about the *GoFundMe* account since September.

Rick never was a technology junkie, but even he must have thought, "Couldn't you have emailed this?" The video was the original *GoFundMe* video appeal and then the "Thank You" video we posted after we blew away our goal. As Rick watched the video, it all came together and he understood, and he began to cry. He got his WalkAide®, a bathroom remodel, and truly even more.

It wasn't quite the Publisher's Clearing House commercial, but there was a check presented and there were lots of tears. It was a truly memorable Thanksgiving Day—made possible by the collective efforts of over two hundred donors and a small band of kids who grew up to be big-time adults with bigger hearts.

What a gift to smile about—$13,087.70!

GOFUNDME
DONATIONS

PART 3

RUNNING AND FUNDRAISING

CHAPTERS 11–15

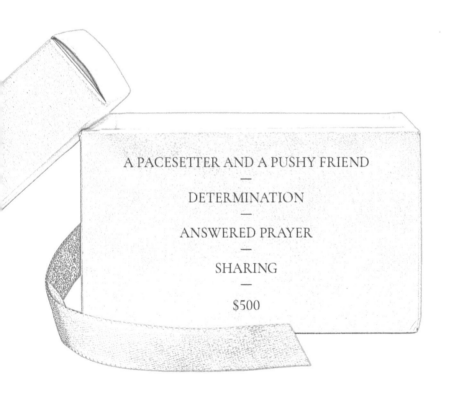

A PACESETTER AND A PUSHY FRIEND
—
DETERMINATION
—
ANSWERED PRAYER
—
SHARING
—
$500

Chapter 11

The Race: "Shut Up and Run"

… Run in such a way as to get the prize.
1 Corinthians 9:24

September 11, 2016. The Big One was finally here. Today I was going to try to break thirty minutes in a 5K (3.1 miles) race. Gary Yeager was going to run with me, using a watch with a GPS app to set and maintain a pace of nine minutes per mile. We had been looking forward to this race since the Steady Strides race in June. My time of 31:36 in that race gave me the incentive to set a 5K goal of under thirty minutes. I figured I was in the best shape I would ever be in, and at sixty-five years old, I wasn't getting any younger. To top it off, I had a progressive, degenerative disease. In my mind, it was now or never.

When I got up that morning, I was sick. I couldn't believe it. I had been training since November, and now I was sick on the day of the race. Terri and I decided she would take me to Gary's anyway, and meet us later at the starting gate. Terri told Gary I was sick, and then prayed for me. Gary just said, "Get in the car." We drove downtown to Sawyer Point where the race was being held. We walked, stretched, and decided we should start the race and see what happened. I couldn't let all the hard training I had done go to waste. I was going to run the race, no matter what. I knew I might have to run at a slower pace, but I was determined to finish the course. Gary said he would run whatever pace I could run.

We finished stretching and went to the starting line. I looked at Gary and blurted out, "Who cares how I feel? After all, what's the worst thing that can happen? I throw up. So what!" And then I said, "Let's go under thirty." Gary encouraged, "Stay with me! We'll do it!"

Just then the gun sounded, and we were off—aiming for that nine-minute pace. At the one-half-mile marker, Gary's watch told us our pace was 9:05. This was a great start. At the one-mile marker, it was 9:04. We were right on, but could we keep it up? As we passed one and a half miles, we were at 8:56. I couldn't believe that we were just under nine minutes. This was the fastest and steadiest pace I had ever run. At the two-mile marker, our pace was 9:05. I was amazed at our consistency. I could sure feel that we were running a fast race. My legs were starting to hurt, and my lungs couldn't seem to get enough air.

But Gary was relentless. At two and a half miles, his watch said 9:15. We needed to pick it up a bit, but I was beginning to slow down and to drop behind. Gary urged me to catch up and stay with him. I reassured him, "Don't worry, I'll make it. This is a really good course. It is flat and fast. The best thing is that there are no hills." Gary looked over his left shoulder and scolded, "Shut up and run." And so I did. Gary then picked up the pace a little and on we ran. I don't know where the energy came from, but I was able to stay with him. When I heard that our three-mile pace was 9:05, with only one-tenth of a mile left to run, I knew we would meet our goal. I was elated. I knew about how many steps it took me to run one-tenth of a mile, so I started counting my steps. This helped me deal with the pain, and boy, was I in pain. I was spent, but Gary just kept up the pace as he encouraged me to hang in there. At two hundred steps I felt I should have finished this race by now, but it seemed like there was still *another* tenth of a mile to run. As we turned the final bend and headed for the finish line, I looked down the home stretch. The official time clock had just turned twenty-nine minutes. This felt like the longest tenth of a mile I'd ever run. But I crossed the finish line at last with a time of 29:27. I was exhausted, but energized. Worn out, but refreshed. Terri was waiting for me at the finish line, talking to a reporter who couldn't believe that anyone with Parkinson's disease could run a 5K race, let alone in under thirty minutes.

A good friend of mine said to me about this race, "Rick, you won the race when you crossed the starting line." I understood what he was saying and I knew he was right. Two years ago, I couldn't run at all and wouldn't even think about starting a 5K race. But in just one and a half years, I'd gone from sixty-three minutes down to twenty-nine minutes for a 5K race. It was a wonderful experience, and I was so glad Gary got to share this special race with me. I couldn't have done it without him. As a matter of fact, Gary checked his watch on Monday morning and it showed that we had actually run 3.25 miles—0.15 miles farther than we were supposed to run. When we averaged our mile pace times, we calculated that our final time for the actual 5K race was 28:05. God had blessed us so much that morning. He reminded me that many times we have not because we ask not. But this time I had prayed and asked for a specific time, and God answered my prayer just as I had asked. "Thank You, Lord, for the gift of a pacesetter, the gift of a friend who pushed me to do my best, and for the renewed gift of running. You blessed me by giving me good health over the summer as I trained for this race. Just think, Lord, I had not run in at least ten years, and I had never competed in a race as an adult. I was sixty five years old, and I had Parkinson's disease. But by Your grace, You enabled me to run a 5K race in a time that was competitive with my friends who do not have Parkinson's disease. You are good all the time."

A PACESETTER
AND
A PUSHY FRIEND

"Shut up and run."

Chapter 12

A Feat with His Feet

by Gary Yeager,
close friend, running partner, and pacesetter

… And let us run with perseverance
the race marked out for us,
Hebrews 12:1

By the grace of God, I have been fortunate to enjoy over forty years of distance running. In that time, I have had a lifetime of experiences, too many to count, but I want to write about a singular experience that ranks up there with the greatest.

I met Rick Iles many years back, when he and his wife began attending our church. At that time, Rick had just been diagnosed with Parkinson's disease, and he was just coming to grips with it. Rick is a very engaging man with many interests and passions; one of those was his shared passion with me on distance running.

One of the symptoms Rick experienced from Parkinson's was keeping him from walking correctly due to muscle imbalance issues. By God's grace, a fellow church member was aware of a device that proved it could alleviate those symptoms, but was very costly. Again, by God's grace, and many generous friends, Rick was able to acquire that device.

Shortly thereafter, a dear church friend passed away suddenly from a heart attack. The following spring, a group of friends, including Rick and myself, walked the Cincinnati Heart Mini 5K in his remembrance. During the walk, I goaded Rick that since he had that new contraption, he should "run" a bit of the distance, and Rick happily accepted the challenge. I think that little instance lit a fire in Rick that he could reclaim some ability to begin running again, and he made a commitment to run the next year's Heart Mini 5K with me. I thought it tremendous that he even wanted to attempt it, but when the race came around he upped the ante by saying he wanted to break forty minutes. Knowing the difficult hills on the course, I said we would try, but it would be a serious challenge. Well, try and succeed he did, coming in with a time of 36:32 minutes, which was truly astounding. However, I haven't gotten to the good part yet.

Some time went by for Rick, with many ups and downs in his running training. In spite of these ups and downs, Rick and I decided to run in the Sunflower Fundraiser 5K race on Sunday, September 11, 2016. The race was downtown at the Riverfront Park. Rick had stated before the race he wanted to beat thirty minutes for the race. Again I thought, we will see if Rick has it in him. With the benefit of using a GPS tracker, we were able to pace Rick throughout the race, and honestly, I have never seen anyone run a gutsier race. Not only did Rick beat thirty minutes, but we actually ran further than the 5K distance to finish! Rick never complained; he just did what he set out to do. That race will always go down in my book of running memories as a testament of what a person can accomplish by putting their mind and determination to it. I am very thankful to have been a part of it.

Unfortunately, Rick has had a string of injuries since that memorable day that has significantly curtailed his ability to run. I have faith, though, that a fulfilling running future is still in store for Rick!

DETERMINATION

Chapter 13

From a Flying Pig to an Unsteady Stride: Prayers and Pain

… they will run and not grow weary, …
Isaiah 40:31

"So I say to you: Ask and it shall be given to you;
seek and you will find; knock and the door will be opened to you."
Luke 11:9

The most popular races in our city are the Flying Pig races. I had always wanted to run the 5K race, but I never had anyone to run with me. Since the Flying Pig was celebrating its twentieth anniversary, I thought it would be a special race to run. I didn't want to run alone, so I prayed that one of my friends would step out and join me.

I decided to ask Jay, a good friend who lives out of town, if he would like to run the 5K race with me. It turns out Jay had been training to run the Flying Pig Marathon, but he was unable to complete his training due to some health issues in his family. I hated to see his training go to waste, and I was excited when he agreed to run with me. Jay is a nut, with a great sense of humor, and I knew he would make the race a lot of fun.

Our goal was to run/walk the race and finish in thirty-six to thirty-eight minutes. We would run one minute and then we would walk one minute. We ran at my running pace and walked at Jay's walking pace (which seemed almost as fast as my running pace). In the middle of the race there were several times when we ran two or three minutes and walked one minute.

It was a fun race. We picked on each other, challenged each other, and were both determined to win the race. We were not going to let the other man pull away and win by a large margin. When we could see the finish line, we decided to cross it together and we actually crossed side by side. Of course, we had the exact same time. It was thirty-six minutes. We just went out and did it. Both of us were satisfied with our time.

We felt our training for the Flying Pig would enable us to run a faster pace in the Steady Strides 5K Fundraiser. We made it our goal to run that race, which was in two weeks, in thirty-two to thirty-six minutes. We said a prayer of thanksgiving for the good race we had just run, and asked God to bless our next race. Little did I know that I wouldn't be able to run that event, and that this Flying Pig 5K would turn out to be my last race.

On Thursday, five days after the Flying Pig race, I fell in my driveway and tore the rotator cuff in my left shoulder. An MRI showed I had actually pulled a small piece of bone off the large bone, and I ripped the muscle off the bone. This was a serious injury, and I needed shoulder surgery to repair the damage. Of course, I would not be running in the Steady Strides race.

I was upset with God. How could He answer one prayer and then allow me to fall and have such a serious injury? Then came the question God is asked the most: "Why?" At first I asked this question with a clenched fist. I was upset God had done this to me. But as I reflected upon how God sees the whole picture, I kept coming back to the fact that God is trustworthy, and if I was going to ask, "Why," I needed to ask with a humble heart.

When I shared this experience with a good friend, she told me when we want to ask God, "Why," we really need to ask God, "Who." She went on to say that God could use any situation He puts us in to show others His grace, mercy, and peace. She believes during difficult times we need to take the spotlight off of ourselves and shine it on others. She knows if we are kind, joyful, patient, thoughtful, and loving, even in the midst of difficulties, the people around us will sit up and take notice. People know this kind of behavior is not natural. It is supernatural, and they will see we have been with Jesus. As I was dealing with the pain and difficulties of rotator cuff surgery, I determined I would show thoughtfulness, kindness, patience, love, and joy, especially to the women at the physical therapy office. (I made everyone in the office a wooden nativity set for Christmas as a way to express kindness and love to each of them.)

When my son Michael heard about my shoulder, he asked what he could do for me. I said his family could pray God would take away the pain I was having and not allow any pain during or after the surgery. I also asked them to pray I wouldn't have pain during the seven months of physical therapy I had to endure. This seemed like a lot to ask, but we all believed God could do it. In fact, God's Word says, *"You do not have, because you do not ask God"* (James 4:2). In our case, God chose to say yes to these prayers. He began by taking away all the pain I was having at that time.

Even more unbelievable, I had no pain after the surgery or during my physical therapy. God answered my family's prayers in a positive way. During the seven months they were praying I would not have pain, I was praying I would be able to run again when my physical therapy was finished. God answered my prayer with what I considered a negative answer. He had taken seven months to answer and His answer was, "No, you will not run again."

I was surprised at how well I took this news. I remembered a short quote I read somewhere. It said we must be willing to give up that which God takes away. I knew God always answers prayer. I needed to trust Him and accept His answer, even if His answer was "No."

I decided to redirect my prayers and pray for my friends and family who were on my team for the Steady Strides 5K race. I prayed they would train well, and run to the best of their ability without getting injured. God faithfully allowed everyone to have a good race without injuries. I also prayed my team would reach our goal for the fundraiser. We came up a little short, but we raised $2,721. That was about $1,000 more than the last year. Once again, some of our prayers were answered, "Yes," and some were answered, "No."

Finally, back to my rotator cuff. As I stated before, I did not have pain during the seven months after surgery. My doctors couldn't believe it. They wanted to know how this could be, and I told them my grandchildren were praying I would not have pain. The doctors just shook their heads and went on with their examination. They didn't know what to think, but they couldn't deny the fact that I was not having any pain.

Then, just two weeks after being released from physical therapy, I fell again and ripped the same muscle in my shoulder. This time, the doctor said I needed a shoulder replacement. Again, I asked my son, his wife, and my grandchildren to pray I would not have pain caused by this injury. God chose to answer this prayer, "Yes," just as he had their last prayer. Once again, I did not have any pain before or after the surgery.

As I thought about how their prayers had been answered, I prayed, "Lord, thank You for the gift of answered prayer. It's not easy to accept an answer of 'No.' My suffering has taught me, no matter what the circumstances, You are always trustworthy. I just wish You would let me run."

ANSWERED
PRAYER

Chapter 14

Crossing the Finish Line Twenty-Eight Times

Rejoice always, pray continually,
give thanks in all circumstances;
for this is God's will for you in Christ Jesus.
1 Thessalonians 5:16–18

On August 23, 2019, I celebrated my fourteenth anniversary of being diagnosed with Parkinson's disease. Wow! Did I really say celebrated? Yes, I did, and I had a lot to celebrate. The disease was progressing very slowly and my medicines were working well. I had a lot of support from family and friends, my wife and children being my biggest fans. I was blessed with the opportunity to meet some wonderful people—many of them battling Parkinson's disease—along with their caregivers and some of their supportive friends. I had the privilege of establishing friendships with many compassionate people in the Parkinson's community. Also, I wrote a Christmas devotional which was published in the fall of 2019. Indeed, I had much to celebrate.

During those fourteen years, God answered many of my prayers in a favorable way. One such prayer was my desire to run again. As you read in Chapter 12, a friend of mine had a heart attack and died unexpectedly. As a way to honor him, several couples I know decided to walk in the Heart Mini 5K fundraiser in downtown Cincinnati. In that race, in March of 2015, I walked the course very slowly. It took me sixty-three minutes to complete the race. After completing this course, I decided that with my new WalkAide®, I would try to run a 5K. I trained hard for the next year, and in September of 2016, I ran the Sunflower 5K in 28:05. I had taken thirty-five minutes off my time. This was unbelievable. My running partner, Gary, was overwhelmed. Between March 2015 and August 2019, I walked or ran in six 5K races. I was thrilled by the fact that even though I had Parkinson's disease, I could run again with my friends.

However, this achievement was minor compared to my role in the Steady Strides 5K races during the last six years. In each of those years, God gave me the gift of a team of runners and walkers who supported me, challenged me, and pushed me to do my very best. They not only walked or ran the race, but they also recruited their friends as racers and donors. I was amazed by the growth of my team, both in the number of people who walked/ran, and in the amount of money they raised.

My team grew from twenty-five people in 2016 to 126 people in 2021. In 2018, my friends brought fourteen people who didn't even know me. How fun it was to meet and walk/run with the friends of my friends. I was injured in 2019 and I couldn't run the race. I was afraid I would lose some of my teammates, but my team rallied around me and continued to grow. Not only did the size increase, but so did the money, going from $1,100 in 2016 to $8,502 in 2021. I was thrilled and humbled by the willingness of everyone to put so much effort into building up our team and raising so much money.

In 2019, I asked myself what I could do to show my appreciation and gratitude to each member of my team. I decided I would meet each of them about fifty yards from the finish line, run or walk with them, and cross the finish line together. As we ran/walked the homestretch, I thanked them for being on my team and told them how much I appreciated their willingness to invest their time and talents in this race. After we crossed the finish line, I'd hurry back out on the course so I could meet my next team member and cross the finish line with them. I hoped this short run with me showed the team every person was just as important to me as the fastest runner and the largest donor.

There were fifty-five people on my team who finished the race, and I crossed the finish line with fifty-one of them. I crossed the line twenty-eight times, sometimes with one runner, and many times with a small group who had stayed together. Almost everyone thanked me for allowing them to be on my team. Later, many of them said the best part of the day was when I ran or walked with them for that last fifty yards. They said it was special (spelled with a capital S).

When asked why it was so special to have me finish the race with them, one runner said it was a way that I could share the journey with my team members. He knew I couldn't run the entire way, so he ran most of the race for me, and he was so blessed when I finished it with him. Another runner said he was there to support me, but then realized I was there to support him. He said running the last part together made it seem like we had done the whole race together. A runner who was injured complained about his hamstring tightening up and his feet hurting. But, running the last fifty yards with me, as I laughed at his jokes, made him forget the "agony of de feet." Finally, my physical therapist said that it showed my determination to not give up, but to be able to change my goals and to have the foresight to think of others above myself. Perhaps she said it best: "Knowing you, why am I not surprised that you crossed the finish line twenty-eight times?"

As you can see, I have much to celebrate. Truly, I am a blessed man who happens to have Parkinson's disease.

SHARING

Crossing the finish line with Debra, my youngest daughter.

Chapter 15

Can't You Spare $15?

Therefore I tell you,
whatever you ask for in prayer,
believe that you have received it,
and it will be yours.
Mark 11:24

In the middle of August 2020, the Steady Strides committee decided that, due to the strict regulations imposed by the state health department, the fundraiser race would be called off or changed to a virtual race. As a result, almost everyone on the committee believed fundraising would be much harder than before. I was optimistic and said I believed we would reach our goal of $130,000. Having said that, I decided to keep my team goals of gathering one hundred team members and raising $5,000.

On Friday, August 14, I had forty-two team members and had raised $2,485. I told Terri I needed $15 to be halfway to my fundraising goal of $5,000. I could have donated this amount myself, but I decided to pray the Lord would put it on someone's heart to give this small amount. I told Him this would be a blessing to me, to my team, and to the committee. I told Terri I had prayed with the expectation God would answer this prayer quickly, and I was leaving it in His hands. I went to bed confident my prayer would be answered by morning.

When I woke up, the first thing I did was check my team information: still forty-two people and $2,485. I checked several times that day with the same results. I couldn't stop myself from checking one last time before going to bed Saturday evening, but there was still no change.

In the stillness and quietness of my room, I began to talk to the Lord. I told Him I didn't get it. Surely He had $15 to spare. I'd been good. Why wasn't He blessing me? Didn't I deserve better than this? Oh, how quickly our theology changes when God doesn't live up to our standards.

Sunday morning came and the first thing I did was check my team information. It was just as I expected—no change. What was I thinking? How quickly I had gone from a simple prayer of expectation to thinking the Lord was not as trustworthy as I imagined Him to be.

Sunday afternoon, I checked several times and the total was still $2,485. Sunday evening, I checked every thirty minutes, but still no change. I went to bed a little bummed. I told the Lord again that I knew He had $15 to spare, and I reminded Him being halfway to my goal would be a great blessing to me. I just didn't understand.

On Monday morning, I reluctantly went to my computer, opened my team page, and, to my great surprise, God had put it on someone's heart to donate not $15, but $500. I was flabbergasted and could hardly believe it. I looked again. Did it really say $500? Yes, it did. But here's the kicker: I didn't recognize the name of the person who had donated this large amount.

The donor's name was Tom Able (name changed). I wrote down the last name of every Tom I knew, but none of them had the last name of Able. I decided to stop thinking about it; instead, I asked the Lord to help me remember my connection with this person. All of a sudden, it came to me. A man named Tom had recently joined our exercise class.

I found the roster and, sure enough, there he was. I had

befriended Tom when he joined our group two months before. After hearing several of us talking about the good time we'd had at the last fundraiser, he told me he was going to donate to my team. His donation was the largest donation my team received in the five years I'd had a team. I was both overwhelmed and humbled. I realized I had to talk to the Lord, confess to Him my unbelief, and ask His forgiveness.

A few days later, I was sitting in my backyard trying to be still before the Lord, but my mind kept drifting back to the race and the $500. I still couldn't believe it. That's when the Lord spoke to me and said, "Fifteen dollars? You could have put that in yourself. What kind of a blessing is that? I've got so much more to share with my children, above and beyond what they ask. Learn a lesson here: *You have not, because you ask not* (James 4:2). I chose to bless you in a big way. You never thought anyone would ever donate $500, but I put it on Tom's heart to do just that." I began to pray, and I asked this question, "Lord, who am I that you should choose to bless me over and over again? Thank You, Jesus."

I saw Tom a few weeks after this happened. He did not know the story of me asking the Lord for $15. I told him about asking for this specific amount, waiting impatiently, and being disappointed when the Lord didn't answer immediately. I told him I doubted God and had to ask for His forgiveness. Then I shared about my joy and unbelief when I saw he donated $500. I was unaware that after meeting me and hearing I had a team, the Lord put it in his heart to donate. I asked him about the timing of his gift, and he said the Lord told him to give it that weekend.

When I told this story to a friend of mine, he asked me a question that penetrated to the very depths of my being. His question was, "Why did you only ask for $15? God owns all the cattle on a thousand hills (Psalm 50:10), and he is the ultimate gift giver. Ask for more. Don't limit God."

When I told this to Tom, he just laughed and said, "Your friend is right. I'm glad God used me to give you so much more than you asked for. God blessed me by blessing you."

PART 4

DOWN, BUT NOT OUT

CHAPTERS 16–20

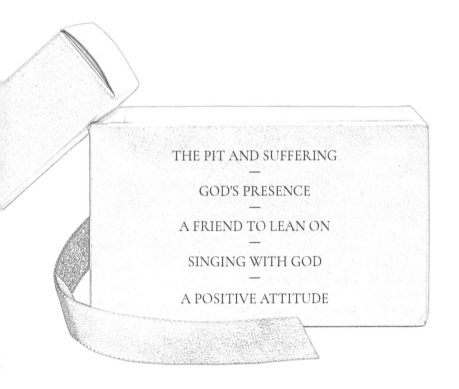

THE PIT AND SUFFERING
—
GOD'S PRESENCE
—
A FRIEND TO LEAN ON
—
SINGING WITH GOD
—
A POSITIVE ATTITUDE

Chapter 16

An Unexpected Pit Stop

He lifted me out of the slimy pit,
out of the mud and mire;
he set my feet on a rock and gave me a firm place to stand.
Psalm 40:2

At this point in my journey with Parkinson's, I had enjoyed many blessings and unexpected victories. I had a lot to celebrate. But how quickly all of this would change over the next three years. During that period of time, I would have six surgeries (two on my shoulder, hernia repair, kidney stone removal, prostate surgery, and back surgery), as well as seven injections into my lower back.

It all began on Monday, July 16, 2018. I was having some dyskinesia and fell in my driveway. I didn't break anything, but I bruised myself in several places. Two days later, some friends came over to help me build some steps next to my garage. While I was squatting down, I lost my balance and reached back to steady myself. My hand landed on a board that had a nail in it and the nail went all the way through the heel of my hand. It was extremely painful. I actually pulled the nail, still attached to the board, out of my hand. The next day, I had a follow-up visit for my rotator cuff surgery, so I showed the surgeon my hand. All I needed was an antibiotic to prevent infection.

Then the next Monday, July 23, my dyskinesia started at 9:40 a.m. and lasted the whole day. I was bouncing off the walls, knocking things over, running into things, and almost falling. It was the worst dyskinesia I'd ever had. I called my neurologist and he said it had to be more than just Parkinson's, so he ordered some lab tests. I had these done on Tuesday and found out I had a urinary tract infection. Who would have ever thought this infection would affect me so much? Over Tuesday, Wednesday, and Thursday, I kept getting worse. I had a reaction to the antibiotics, so the doctor gave me a different medication. After taking it, I began to feel a little better.

On Thursday evening, I went behind the garage to finish the plans for building my new steps. When I was finished, I could barely stand up. I just wanted to get to the house and go to bed. I walked slowly up the hill, but when I reached the top, I began falling back down. It felt like the world was in slow motion. I was moving with little shuffle steps, going backwards all the way down the hill. I couldn't believe I didn't fall to the ground. But once I stopped, I couldn't move. Finally, I dropped to the ground and actually crawled up to the driveway. It started to rain and I was soaked to the skin. I still could not stand up. No one was home, so I crawled, rolled, and did the duck walk, trying to get into the house. My glasses fell off and I stepped on them, breaking them all to pieces.

Not only was it frightening, it seemed to get worse every minute. I'd never felt so helpless in my life. I finally got in the house, where I just collapsed on the floor. I tried to call Terri, but couldn't reach her. Eventually, I crawled into my bedroom and got into my bed. I was totally exhausted.

When Terri pulled into the driveway she knew something was wrong. My tools were still in the driveway, getting soaked by the rain. The hood of my Jeep was open and the engine was covered with water. The lights were on in the garage and there were more tools scattered on the garage floor. Something was definitely wrong. She couldn't find me outside, so she ran into the house and looked for me. When she found me in my room my dyskinesia was so bad I could not stop moving and my whole condition frightened Terri. Thank God, I was finally able to go to sleep.

Then morning came. The new antibiotic kicked in and most of the dyskinesia went away. I had very little dyskinesia again on Saturday. It's remarkable how quickly the right medicine can work. I found out many Parkinson's patients have urinary tract infections and they can cause a lot of problems. Mine was a terrifying experience. I felt like I'd been thrown into a pit and abandoned to wallow around in the mud.

During this ugly time in my life, I still tried to have personal devotions. I had been meditating on 1 Thessalonians 5:17–18, *Pray continually. Give thanks in all circumstances.* After having four very bad days the previous week, I was asking the Lord what there was to be thankful for. Praying wasn't a problem. I had a real need to talk to the Lord, and there was a lot to talk about. But being thankful? That was another story.

I was thinking about this at breakfast on Monday morning, July 30. I felt the Lord telling me to be quiet, to be still in my soul, because He had something to say to me. I believed He was going to answer my question about thankfulness. And He did. He spoke to my heart and said, "In the busyness, frustration, ugliness, unfairness, and even the goodness of life, I may allow you to slip, dive, back up, 'accidentally' fall, or be thrown into a miserable, miry pit. You might throw yourself in, I may put you there, and I may even allow Satan to throw you in. Then, in My own time, I will reach down and grab your outstretched hands and will lift you out of the dark muddy hole and into My light. Then I will cleanse you by washing off the miserable, clinging mud you have been wallowing in. I will cover you with My righteousness. I will walk with you down the path I have chosen for you. Surely you can find something to be thankful for, even when you feel forsaken and left alone."

While pondering what God said, I realized that I did have much to be thankful for. And so I prayed, "Thank You, Father, for the pit. It has given me a greater grasp of Your purposes. It has reminded me of the many ways You work in my life. Also, thank You, Jesus, for delivering me from the pit. I now have a better understanding of how dirty I was before You cleansed me with your blood. When

You brought me out of this miry mud hole, I realized how much Your presence was needed in my life. Thank You for shedding Your blood and for cleansing me. Thank You, Holy Spirit, for going into such a miserable place with me. When I entered the pit, I was not aware that You were with me. But as my heart turned toward Christ, I knew He would never leave me alone. So He sent you into the pit with me. Your presence brought hope in the midst of the pit. Your guidance took me to Jesus. Lord, help me learn from this experience by giving me Word-centered wisdom. Thank You for the gift of suffering in the pit. You are indeed transforming me into the man You want me to be."

THE PIT
AND
SUFFERING

Chapter 17

Lost on a Hike: Together/Alone

The LORD makes firm the steps
of the one who delights in him;
though he may stumble, he will not fall,
for the LORD upholds him with his hand.
Psalm 37:23–24

My son Philip and his Uncle Mike co-own a 120-acre farm near Dry Ridge, Kentucky. It is a pretty remote piece of land. To get to it, you hike about one-half mile on a dirt and gravel road, which ends at some railroad tracks. Their property line is on the opposite side of these tracks. Since there is no road here, you must hike up a steep hill or drive up a rocky creek bed. If you drive, you need a four-wheel-drive vehicle. At the top of this hill is a dirt road which follows the ridge top for about three quarters of a mile, ending in a meadow where we have a small cabin.

We enjoy taking friends there so we can hike, ride four-wheelers, shoot our guns, work in our garden, or just hang out. We have hiked all over these 120 acres and found many unusual and interesting things. We've found the cornerstones for the foundation of a cabin, a dug-out well, old glass bottles, and a circular fruit cellar constructed entirely of rock, even the roof. The farm is also a great place to hunt. While hunting, you have a reason to follow deer trails and really explore the woods. When Philip and I are there, we spend a lot of time alone in the woods. It is a great place to be by yourself, giving you the opportunity to clear your mind and heart, to be still, and to communicate with the Lord. We tell our friends this is a place where you can be with someone, but you can be together/alone ... or should we say alone/together?

Over the course of the last year, I asked CW, a good friend and an avid hiker, if he would like to go to the farm and hike with me. He had said yes, but the weather was not cooperating, and we could not find a good time to go. Finally, during a string of some beautiful spring days, we hastily set up a day to go hiking.

I told CW all about the farm during the hour and ten minutes it took to drive there. I told him our favorite thing to do was spend some time alone each day we were there. I didn't tell him part of my agenda for this day was for both of us to spend between thirty and sixty minutes sitting alone in the woods. We would be within shouting distance of each other, yet we would be together/alone.

When we reached Dove Road, we parked the car and began the first part of our hike. It was already ninety-two degrees with ninety percent humidity. Where did our wonderful spring weather go? Obviously, the string of beautiful days ended the day before. Not wanting to become dehydrated, we loaded our backpacks with all of our water and some chocolate bars.

The first half mile of our hike was on an old roadbed that was level and easy to walk on. At the end of this trail, we had to cross some railroad tracks. I told CW to notice the huge culvert under the tracks. It is big enough for a person to walk through. A man who owned land on the other side of the tracks always walked through this culvert to get to his property.

After we crossed the railroad tracks, the trail became a small creek bed that was rough and steep. The climb was strenuous. When we got to the top of the hill, we were drenched in sweat and needed a break. We drank some water and rested our legs. While sitting there, I decided to get off the roadbed and follow a deer trail down into the valley. This would keep us out of the sun, and I would be able to show CW the well, the cellar, and the cabin foundation. But, after following the deer trail, I couldn't find these things.

We followed deer tracks deep into the woods. I went farther on
the deer trail than I should have, and continued even after I realized
I was in unfamiliar territory. When I spotted an old barn, I knew
we weren't on our property. I was lost, but not lost, knowing that
if we hiked downhill we would get to the main creek bed. Then we
could walk down the creek until we found the culvert.

I could tell my last dose of Sinemet, which I take every three
hours, was wearing off. I hoped that CW hadn't noticed, but he
told me later that he saw I was struggling when we were on the
deer trail. I told him several times that when we got to the creek we
could walk downstream to find the huge culvert. Then we would
know exactly where we were. I kept saying this not for CW's sake,
but to reassure myself.

We found another deer trail and followed it into the brush once
again. We were covered with sweat, running out of water, and
getting scratched by the brambles. We followed this trail for what
seemed like an eternity and finally reached the creek. I thought, *If
we could just get to the culvert, this terrible ordeal could come to
an end.*

CW decided he would hike ahead and look for the culvert
while I rested and waited for my new dose of medicine to kick in.
I watched him carefully picking his way down the creek bed until
suddenly he disappeared around a bend in the creek. As I sat on the
edge of the creek, I realized I was totally alone.

Normally I would enjoy this sense of aloneness, but this time
I became frightened. I began to breathe heavily. My mind started
to race with negative questions. What if we had to spend the night
out here? Would CW find the culvert? What about my meds? Was
CW all right? Was he scared? Did he feel alone? These questions
made me more anxious and I began to feel panicky. After about
ten minutes, which seemed like an hour, CW suddenly reappeared
and gave me a thumbs-up signal. I felt confident he had found the
culvert.

It took ten minutes for him to get back to me. When I stood up, I was very shaky. I had to hold onto CW's backpack to walk through the slippery creek bed. I fell nine or ten times. Each time it was more like a slow motion sit-down than a fall. We were both scared, but we knew where the culvert was and if we reached it, we would be out of the woods—in more ways than one. I was spent, but kept going.

When we reached the culvert, we rested for about five minutes. Then, in a last burst of energy, CW told me to grab his backpack, and he practically dragged me through the culvert. We had just enough room to stand in the culvert, and he pulled me along until we reached the end. I felt like it was as hard on him as it was on me, but we made it.

At the end of the culvert was a small pool. CW was afraid I would fall in. But by now my medicines had kicked in, and I was a little better. I wouldn't let CW help me climb around the water. I assured him that I was not going to fall in, and I managed to make it. We walked up a small hill and went down the main road to his car.

This hike turned out to be a scary adventure. We didn't get to see the cabin foundation, the well, or the cellar. CW didn't get to enjoy the hike. But he was gracious with me. He stayed with me, encouraged me, carried me, and supported me during this horrible hike. He was surprised to see me mentally shut down and be so physically spent that I was struggling to even walk. When we saw his car, I said, "Thank the Lord! This is over!" These simple words brought tears to my eyes because I had gone through this whole ordeal without praying. How stupid could I be?

The next day, I was sitting in my backyard thinking about the hike and all of the things I had done wrong. I couldn't believe that when I realized we had gone the wrong way, I didn't think to pray and ask the Lord to guide us to the path we should be on. I was still puzzled by my fear when CW disappeared around the bend. I never expected to be frightened while being alone. I had forgotten that I never am truly alone, for God has said, *"Never will I leave you, never will I forsake you"* (Hebrews 13:5). I wondered why I didn't remember this while we were hiking. As I sat there, I whispered a simple prayer. "Lord, thank You for watching over CW and me on our hike yesterday. Thank You for the gift of Your presence, even though we didn't think to pray, nor did we recognize You were with us the entire day. You came to our aid and protected us on this horrible hike. You are certainly a trustworthy God."

GOD'S PRESENCE

Chapter 18

A Shared Adventure

by CW Spencer,
good friend, fellow author, and fellow teacher

Two are better than one,
because they have a good return for their labor:
If either of them falls down, one can help the other up. …
Ecclesiastes 4:9–10

Rick and I picked an extremely hot, humid day to hike on his family's farm in Grant County. But that was okay; this would only be a couple of miles or so, up to the top of the ridge and back. Besides, I like spending time with Rick, and we had talked about this hike for a long time.

We had a couple of snack bars and about a liter of water each. Not much, but for a couple of miles we figured we'd be good. We started by walking a quarter mile until we crossed the railroad tracks. Then, instead of following the dirt lane up to the farmhouse, Rick decided we'd bushwhack up the hill through the trees instead.

We immediately entered thick undergrowth. It was very slow going; it must have taken two hours to find our way through the sticky brambles up to the ridgetop. We were soaked with sweat and covered with scratches when we reached the top.

There was a barn of some sort where we came out, but Rick didn't recognize it. We walked around in the clearing to try to find something that looked familiar, but nothing did. We decided to head back into the woods and down the hill. Water was getting scarce and Rick seemed to be shakier. We would find the creek and follow it down. I asked Rick if he was sure this was the place to enter the woods again. He said yes, but I had this feeling he was not sure.

After a half hour, we were at the creek. But instead of following it down, Rick pointed west and said he knew the way. It was more or less uphill. I was puzzled at the change of plans. But Rick is one of the smartest and most capable men I know. We turned west and left the creek. I was worried at how Rick was shaking, and kept checking that he was taking his medicine.

After forty-five minutes of wandering, I finally spoke up when I spotted the creek again. I insisted we get down to it and follow it downstream as originally planned. It was evening now. Our drinking water was gone and we had no filtration supplies. Mosquitoes had found us. I worried about having to stay overnight and about Rick's medicine supply.

By now, Rick was shaking as bad as I'd ever seen and having trouble walking, let alone navigating through the woods. Rick would offer directions, but didn't seem sure and yielded to my suggestions. (It wasn't until the next day Rick told me that by that time he had been losing touch with reality.) We reached the creek and sat down. At this point, Rick was practically unable to walk on his own. I told him to rest and I'd head downstream and find the culvert.

Rick is someone who, before Parkinson's, roamed these hills at will on hunting trips. That day I saw the devastating toll this disease takes. I tried not to panic, but I rushed downstream as fast as I could.

I was overjoyed to see the culvert in about ten minutes. It was narrower and longer than I had hoped, but I saw no way we would be able to cross the tracks on the high ridge they followed.

I headed back to Rick. He was sitting and seemed confused.

We decided he would hold on to my pack and follow me down the creek. He was shaking badly. We followed the creek bed, but occasionally had to climb the bank. This took everything Rick had to hang on. I was full of adrenaline and had no problem pulling.

It took a long half hour to get to the culvert. We had to duck while I assisted Rick through it. No easy task for either of us. At the end was a pond that had to be navigated around. Here, Rick seemed clear-headed, and said strongly and clearly he would do it himself. I deferred, ready to jump in and pull him out if need be. But he pulled it all together and made it to safety. We walked down the level lane back to the car.

After the air conditioner kicked on and we downed some snacks and fluids at a nearby convenience store, Rick started to get his bearings back. I felt bad that the day had been so crazy and that I hadn't stepped in sooner, but mostly I felt great relief that my friend was getting back to himself. And, I learned some lessons that might come in handy on our next hike.

I had felt sorry for Rick at times that day, but as usual, he wasn't feeling sorry for himself. In fact, he has said more than once that he wouldn't trade his Parkinson's now. That disease has created opportunities for him that he would never have had without it.

I know one thing: Rick is a huge inspiration to me.

A FRIEND
TO LEAN ON

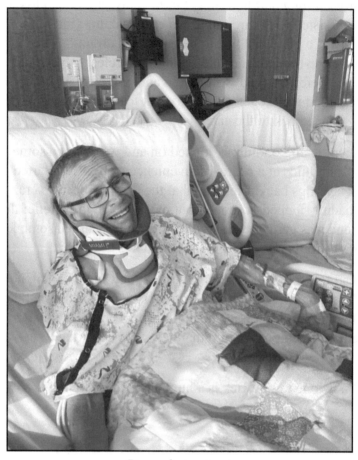

Down, but not out.

Chapter 19

Singin' in the Pain

You are my hiding place;
you will protect me from trouble
and surround me with songs of deliverance. (emphasis added)
Psalm 32:7

The month of February 2021 was not good to me. From February 3 through February 8, I had not slept well because of intense pain in my right hip. I hated to wake up in the morning because my pain got worse when I tried to stand up. No matter what I did, the pain would not go away.

On Monday, February 8, I was sitting on the foot of my bed, unable to move because of pain shooting down my legs. When I tried to get up, the pain was horrible. All I wanted to do was get to the head of my bed and get under the covers. I was really struggling. It seemed as if I was moving only an inch at a time. It took me about fifteen minutes to get where I wanted to be. As I was struggling, I realized that for the past few minutes I had been subconsciously singing the chorus of a hymn I learned as a child. The hymn is titled "Without Him." I was singing these words:

> Without Him I could do nothing,
> Without Him I'd surely fail,
> Without Him I would be drifting,
> Like a ship without a sail.

Jesus, Oh Jesus, Do you know Him today,

Do not turn Him away,

Oh Jesus, My Jesus,

Without Him, how lost I would be.[1]

As I sang the verse again, I said to myself, I've done this before. I remembered that just two weeks earlier, I had a similar experience. That morning I couldn't get out of bed and walk to the kitchen. It was too painful to straighten out my legs. As I was struggling, I noticed I was singing another old hymn. I wasn't consciously singing it. It was just playing out in my mind. The song is titled "My Savior's Love."

I stand amazed in the presence,

Of Jesus the Nazarene,

And wonder how He could love me,

A sinner condemned unclean.

Oh, how marvelous!

Oh, how wonderful!

And my song shall ever be;

Oh, how marvelous!

Oh, how wonderful!

Is my Savior's love for me![2]

Later that day as I thought about these two instances, I was reminded of the movie and the song, *Singin' in the Rain*. It seemed as if the Holy Spirit said, "You weren't singing alone this morning. We, you and I, were singing in the pain." Then He whispered, "Did you notice I changed the word rain to pain?" I couldn't wrap my head and heart around this wonderful gift; God and I were singing

1   Mylon LeFevre, "Without Him," Angel Band Music (BMI; admin at CapitolCMGPublishing.com), 1963. All rights reserved. Used by permission.

2   Charles H. Gabriel, "My Savior's Love" (public domain).

together in the midst of pain. I thought there must be a deeper or hidden meaning in all of this. Indeed, there was!

An article on GradeSavers.com titled "Singin' in the Rain: Symbols, Allegory, and Motifs" says:

> The lyrical content of the song expresses the notion that even though the weather might be inclement and dreary, Lockwood feels happy and unflappable. His motivation for dancing unprotected and in a torrential downpour is having realized that the woman he loves feels the same way. Lockwood feels so good that nothing can get him down, not even the unpleasantness of the storm. Thus, the storm becomes the symbol of hardship and the less enjoyable parts of life. Lockwood's blissful impulse to sing in the rain serves as an act of rebellion against darkness. His singing represents Lockwood's optimism which carries him through difficult situations.[3]

I found I could easily use the symbols discussed by these authors to share my story of living with the storms of Parkinson's disease. I've certainly faced inclement and dreary weather since being diagnosed with this chronic illness on August 23, 2005. The storms of this hideous disease have included dystonia (cramping of my foot), extreme fatigue, low blood pressure, fainting, being at risk to fall, actually falling, loss of fine motor skills, and loss of cognitive skills.

Sometimes, in the midst of these storms, thunder and lightning have reared their ugly heads in the form of surgeries. From June 2018 through April 2021, I have had six surgeries. Those include: a left shoulder rotator cuff repair, nine months later a left shoulder replacement, lower spine fusion, a hernia repair, prostate surgery, and kidney stone surgery. (I had a kidney stone the size of a racquetball).

During those same years, I had intense pain in my lower back, and I had seven injections which should have relieved this pain.

---

3   GradeSaver "Singin' in the Rain, Symbols, Allegory and Motifs." Grade-Saver 4, July, 2022. Web. 4 July 2022.

They didn't work. As you can see, those three years of my life were filled with doctor visits, many diagnostic tests, and several surgeries. The storms were frequent and heavy.

However, God is trustworthy. I have the promise that I don't have to fear because God is holding me with His right hand, and He is rejoicing over me with singing (Isaiah 41:13 and Zephaniah 3:17). Certainly, that is a gift we can sing about. We should have joy because the Lord is so active in our lives. Nothing can separate us from God's love, so we can be unflappable as we sing in the pain. The darkness of our spiritual enemies must be defeated, and one way to do that is to always be "Singin' in the (Pain)." God will join us in our song!!! What a tremendous and overwhelming gift, singing with God. I have learned our optimism and our trust in God, coupled with the fact the Lord is completely trustworthy, will carry us through difficult experiences. Our dependence on the Lord draws us away from sin and on to sainthood. This is my prayer: "Lord, enable me to remember to sing in the pain, and please join me."

SINGING
WITH GOD

Chapter 20

I Miss Superman

By Philip Iles, the author's oldest son

Be on your guard; stand firm in the faith;
be courageous; be strong.
Do everything in love.
1 Corinthians 16:13–14

My Papa, my hero, my own personal Superman. The strongest man alive; he taught me it is possible to do anything just by trying. Teacher, painter, story-teller, church camp director, church choir director, youth group leader, Sunday school teacher, home improvement guru, comedian, great all-around athlete.

He's the guy that you want on your team because he always rises to the competition, no matter the sport.

As a boy, I was always helping Dad with projects around the house. I held the wood while he sawed and the flashlight when he worked on the car. I rode along to the hardware store when he needed supplies. My Grandpa Iles was a Baptist minister and when he was diagnosed with cancer, Dad took over the Wednesday night services for him and I was there with him. The car conversations were always something to look forward to. I remember sitting in the front seat and sticking my tongue out and him snatching it in his hand. He took me and three friends on in basketball once and beat all of us. Allen, one of his former students, exclaimed, "Mr.

Iles, you can jump!"

When I asked if we could start hunting deer at age fourteen, Dad jumped at the chance. We'd drive to Adams County late Friday night and hunt on our friend Jerry's property.

We camped often at the creek—fishing, shooting, playing ball, hiking, and riding bikes.

We've always shared books, both loving American history and good fiction.

I remember the summer Dad came home early from church camp. He looked terrible and it was obvious he was not well. He was moving slowly and having trouble completing thoughts. His hands wouldn't do what he wanted. Something was obviously wrong. He had suddenly slowed down.

After ruling out everything, we discovered he had Parkinson's disease. The man who was never sick now had a chronic, debilitating condition. His plan to teach for thirty-five years and then retire to do something with his hands had to be reevaluated. Somehow he remains positive, he still hasn't stopped. He always has multiple projects going. His trust in God is strong and while he's slowed down, he is always moving forward with a positive attitude.

My Papa, my hero, is still my personal Superman. He may no longer be the strongest man alive, but he is my inspiration. He's my best friend, my rock, my sounding board. He is eternally positive, always thinking of others.

A POSITIVE ATTITUDE

EPILOGUE

by Phill Frye,
Rick's best friend for fifty-two years

Rick's life has been a reflection of the love, compassion, wisdom, and mind of God. He has always been a hero figure to me. Parkinson's only changed his cape for a cane. He has shown greater strength, more compassion, and intense patience while wearing his new superhero outfit.

The gift of Parkinson's has made it possible for him to receive wonderful God-given gifts. Each gift has been given to Rick just when he needed it; not a moment too soon, nor a moment too late. The gifts of the WalkAide®, home renovation, physician diagnosis, encouraging words, trust, grace, and many others, were all given at exactly the right time.

As Rick continues his remarkable journey, we will be blessed as he recognizes and shares the new gifts God has for him. In words Rick used for many years when telling bedtime stories to seven-, eight-, and nine-year-old children at church camp, we can rest assured that God's gifts to Rick are:

"To be!! ... continued."

ACKNOWLEDGMENTS

Thanks be to God. Praise the Lord! He has given me a faith-based hope as I battle Parkinson's disease, and as I look forward to the challenges and victories He has prepared for me.

The Lord has chosen to bless me through many different individuals, beginning with my wife, Terri. She has read the entire manuscript to me. She has provided insights which have made the stories fit together so well. She has been quick to recognize the gifts God has given to us. She is my biggest fan.

My children have contributed to the writing of this book. Philip, my oldest son, wrote the final chapter as a short summary of my life and as a tribute to me. My other son, Michael, designed the book cover. My daughters have always kept up with my progress on the book and they have always encouraged me to "get it done."

I owe so much to my friend Larry Blundred. His bullying, his constant challenges to start writing, and his encouragement through the whole process of writing this book have been invaluable. If he had not pursued me and kept telling me I had a story God wanted me to write, there would not be a book. He seems as excited as I am to see the book in print.

CW and Bonnie Spencer deserve a huge thank-you. I initially asked them to read and edit two chapters and give me some feedback as to the content, the story line, and the grammar. After reading those chapters, they said they would do two more chapters. They ended up doing the whole book. Their hard work is reflected in the easy readability of the text. Just like Larry, they are excited to see the finished book.

I am indebted to Rob Pinkston, Charlie Fehrman, Gary Yeager, CW Spencer, Phill Frye, and Philip Iles for their contributions in writing their side of the story.

Karis Pratt, my editor, has been a delight to work with. She has always welcomed my questions and always given me good reasons for her comments and suggestions. She has displayed a lot of patience when I could not work on the book due to complications with my Parkinson's disease. I'm glad God put us together so this book could be published.

Made in United States
Troutdale, OR
08/19/2024

22156809R00066